Ancient Greece

by Sean Stewart Price

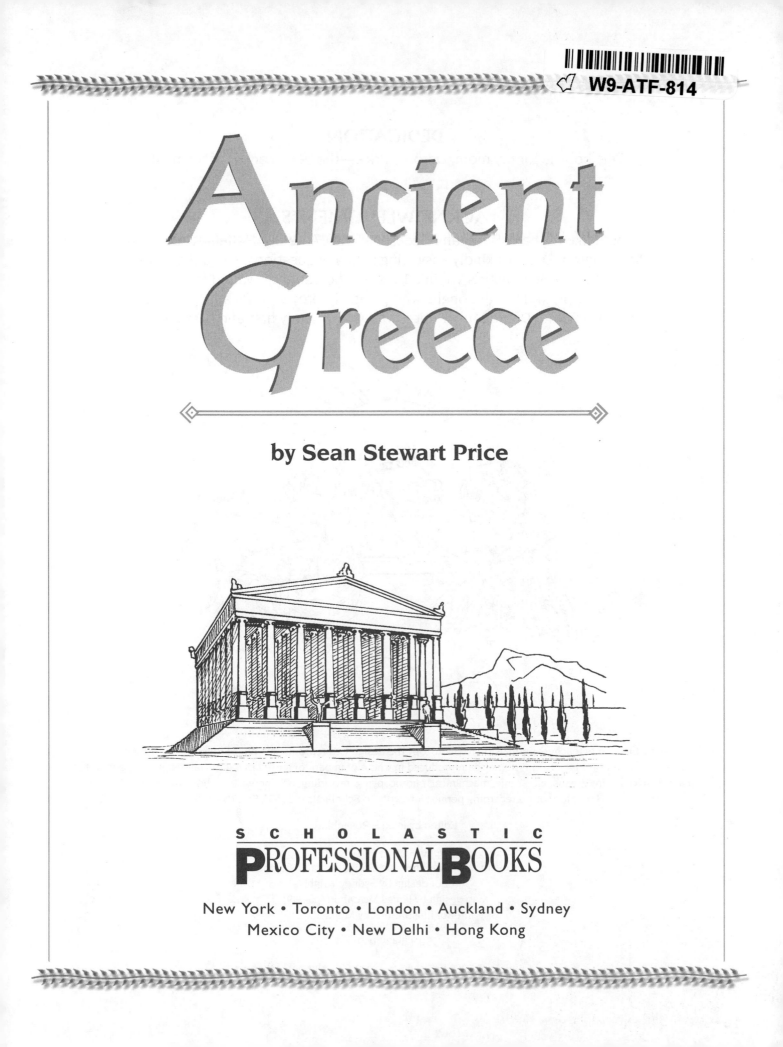

SCHOLASTIC
PROFESSIONAL BOOKS

New York • Toronto • London • Auckland • Sydney
Mexico City • New Delhi • Hong Kong

DEDICATION

This book is for my mom, Dorothy Price—the best teacher of them all.

✦ ✦ ✦ ✦ ✦ ✦ ✦ ✦ ✦ ✦ ✦ ✦ ✦ ✦ ✦

ACKNOWLEDGMENTS

I would like to thank Deborah Boedeker at the Center for Hellenic Studies in Washington, D.C., for kindly answering so many questions. I would also like to thank Scholastic's Virginia Dooley, who patiently waited for the manuscript, and Sarah Longhi, who greatly improved it. Finally, I'd like to thank my wife, Debra Muller Price, who is always my first and best editor.

Edited by Jeanne Rosenblatt

Cover design by Norma Ortiz
Cover photo by John Verde, Photo Researchers, Inc.
Interior design by Sydney Wright
Map design by James McMahon (page 9)
Interior illustrations by Mona Mark

ISBN 0-439-05919-4

Contents

Introduction

⤳ Ancient Greece is not some obscure place in the past—it is all around us. ⤳

If you turn on the TV and watch a drama, you are enjoying an art form invented by the Greeks more than 2,500 years ago. If you pick up a book, each page contains Greek words and concepts. If you visit a doctor, it's likely that he or she took an oath based on one written by Hippocrates, the greatest healer in the ancient world. Visit Washington, D.C., and you'll be struck by the Greek architectural influence on the White House and the Lincoln Memorial. While you're there, you can thank the Greeks for developing ideals of free speech and democracy. But you don't really have to go anywhere to appreciate Greece. On any cloudless night you can look up and be dazzled by the 88 constellations, most of which have names derived from Greek mythology.

Our debt to ancient Greece is enormous. The few things that the Greeks didn't invent or pioneer they greatly improved upon. They knew that they were special and that the eyes of history (another Greek innovation) were upon them. "Future ages will wonder at us," the politician Pericles boasted of Athens, the greatest of the Greek cities, "as the present age wonders at us now."

⤳ Why study ancient Greece? ⤳

Ancient Greece is often called the cornerstone of Western civilization. The examples above give just a hint of the extent to which American culture has been influenced by ancient Greece. Yet an American plopped down in ancient Greece would quickly suffer culture shock. Ancient Greek society was based on agriculture and the use of slaves. It was heavily male-dominated—a society that institutionalized the exclusion of women, foreigners, and people with disabilities from positions of power. The Greeks did not even call themselves Greeks; that word comes from their Latin name. Lumped all together as a people, they called themselves "Hellas." As individuals, they were (and are today) "Hellenes."

We don't study ancient Greece just because it has given us cool ideas and traditions or because some of its customs seem strange and outdated. Instead, we study ancient Greece, as journalist Peter France put it, "because this astonishing people, small in numbers, politically disorganized, poverty-stricken, technologically underdeveloped, suddenly discovered, in their remote corner of the Mediterranean, in a burst of light, how to live." Indeed, studying this culture with our students can become an epic journey with more peaks and valleys than the mountainous Greek countryside.

∽ *About this book* ∽

The materials in this resource invite students to appreciate and learn about ancient Greece— its geography, its history, its culture, and its impact on modern life. Each chapter opens with background information on a specific aspect of ancient Greece and is followed by related activities that help students understand key ideas presented in the chapter. The first chapter aims to give students an understanding of where Greece is located and how the ancient civilization developed there. The subsequent chapters highlight details of Greek culture and everyday life: how people dressed, what they ate, how they entertained themselves, what they thought about, and how they ran their governments.

As you lead students through their study of ancient Greece, be sure to use the enclosed fold-out map, which shows the extent of Greece's political domain around 600 B.C. Point out to the class that Greek colonies stretched from the coast of Spain to the Black Sea. Also encourage the class to explore some of the Internet sites described in the 'Net Links sections of this book and visit your school or local library to obtain some of the books and videos listed in the Library Links sections.

A WARNING ABOUT WEB SITES

Many Web sites about ancient civilizations contain material or links to material that some parents might find objectionable. Before asking your students to investigate a Web site, be sure you have checked it out yourself and determined that it is appropriate.

Web addresses also may change or disappear. If an address doesn't take you where you want to go, retype it using only the domain (e.g., www.scholastic.com) and navigate from the home page to the desired pages by clicking on topics. Or use a search engine to search for key words in the address or Web-site topic.

The Lincoln Memorial
Washington, D.C.

The Parthenon
Athens, Greece

CHAPTER 1

Master of the Ancient Seas

The Geography of Ancient Greece

Modern Greece is about the size of Alabama. You can see from the map on page 9 that most of its land lies at the tip of Europe's Balkan Peninsula. The rest of the country is made up of hundreds of islands that lie scattered throughout four bodies of water: the Aegean Sea, the Ionian Sea, the Mediterranean Sea, and the Sea of Crete.

Although Greece is small in size, its mild climate attracts millions of tourists each year. Most rainfall comes during the winter months, when temperatures seldom dip below freezing. The summers are hot and dry. That forecast has not changed much since Greek culture first emerged, around 2000 B.C.

Most of the great city-states of ancient Greece, such as Athens, Sparta, and Corinth, existed within the borders of modern Greece. But in ancient times—especially during Greece's "Golden Age" in the 5th century B.C.—Greek colonies stretched from the Iberian Peninsula to the Black Sea. The map on page 7 shows the breadth of the Greek territories around 550 B.C.

Two geographic facts help explain why the ancient Greeks spread themselves out over such a broad area. First, their homeland is extremely mountainous and rocky, with most of the farmland relegated to a few fertile valleys and strips along the seacoast. Second, nearly all of Greece was no more than one or two day's travel from the sea. As a result, the sea became Greece's lifeline and, ultimately, its source of power and greatness. The Greeks traded their abundant supplies of limestone, clay pottery, and olives for grain, linen, and papyrus from other Mediterranean peoples. Because the winter months brought shipwrecking storms, most trading took place between April and October.

Athens in particular profited from the necessity for trade. The people there made it easy for foreigners to sail into their seaport of Piraeus loaded down with valuable cargo. The wealth generated by this booming trade helped fund the Golden Age of Greece.

Profit relied on safe trade, and safe trade relied on seamen who knew where they were going. The Greeks did not invent maps. But they did come up with ideas to make maps more useful, such as *latitude* and *longitude*. The philosopher and astronomer Anaximander drew the first known map of the world in the 6th century B.C. Claudius Ptolemy, the last of the great Greek mapmakers, compiled an eight-volume "Geography" around A.D. 150. It exhaustively mapped more than 8,000 specific places in the known world and remained influential throughout the Middle Ages.

The sea helped to shape Greece's culture. Its greatest mythological heroes, such as Jason and Odysseus, spent much of their lives on ships. Many great Greek thinkers, like Anaximander and Ptolemy, did not live in Athens or other mainland cities. They lived in far-flung places—Anaximander and Ptolemy lived in Miletus and Alexandria, respectively—but they were Greeks nonetheless. Their influence spread throughout the Mediterranean due to the traffic of slow, stubby trading ships that made Greece first a superpower and later the cultural heart of the Mediterranean.

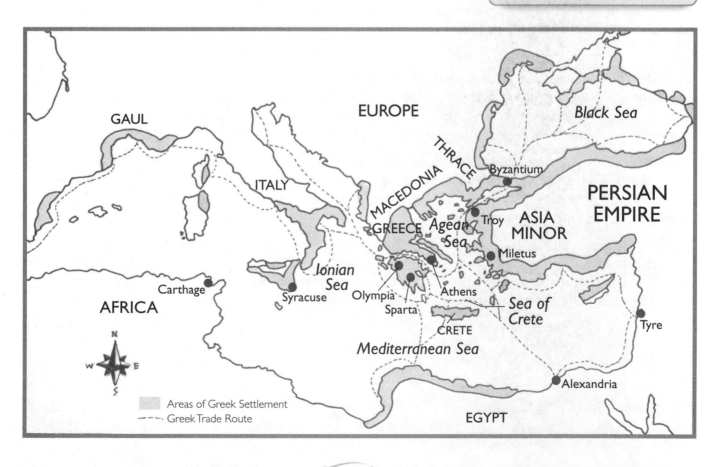

Areas of Greek Settlement
- - - Greek Trade Route

Finding Your Way Around
~ Latitude and Longitude ~

The ancient Greeks invented the mapping system we know today as latitude and longitude. The system developed gradually, starting around the 4th century B.C. Over the next four centuries, astronomers and mapmakers developed their ideas and made the system more exact. Around A.D. 100, latitude and longitude lines were finally laid out at regular, mathematically spaced intervals more or less as they are today. In modern times, latitude and longitude have become the framework for almost all maps. They are also used for high-tech direction-finding satellites that can tell travelers instantly where they are.

MATERIALS

Finding Your Way Around (page 9)

HERE'S HOW

1 Distribute a copy of page 9 to each student.

2 Review the information about latitude and longitude described below.

3 After they have finished the activity sheet, have students figure out the latitude and longitude of their hometown by looking at a state map.

◆ ◆

Latitude: This measures distance north or south of the equator. The equator is an imaginary line that circles the globe halfway between the North and South poles. Latitude lines are called parallels, because they run parallel to (never meet) the equator. The equator is at 0° latitude. Latitude increases as you go north (N) and south (S) of the equator—to 90°N at the North Pole and 90°S at the South Pole.

Longitude: This measures distance east or west of the prime meridian. The prime meridian is an imaginary line that runs from pole to pole and passes through Greenwich, England. All longitude lines are called meridians, and they all meet at the poles. The prime meridian is at 0° longitude. Longitude increases as you travel east (E) and west (W) until you reach the 180° meridian, which is in the Pacific Ocean.

Explain to students that latitude and longitude lines on a map form a grid that allows you to find any spot on earth. Remind them that both latitude and longitude are measured in degrees and that latitude is always given first. For instance, we would say that New Orleans is located at 30°N, 90°W. Finally, point out that to make a location more exact, a degree can be divided into 60 minutes (60').

◆ ◆

ANSWER KEY *Finding Your Way Around* (page 9)

1. parallels; 2. meridians; 3. equator; 4. prime meridian; 5. Crete; 6. Ionian Sea; 7. Peloponnesus, or the Peloponnesian Peninsula; 8. island of Lesbos; 9. island of Rhodes; 10. Athens

Name _____   Date _____

Finding Your Way Around

You'll need to look at the maps below and review what you've learned about latitude and longitude to answer these questions.

1 What is another name for lines of latitude?
_____

2 What is another name for lines of longitude? _____

3 Latitude measures distance from what imaginary line on the globe?
_____

4 Longitude measures distance from what imaginary line on the globe?
_____

5 If you were standing at 35°N, 25°E, where would you be? _____

6 What body of water would you be in at 37°N, 20°E? _____

7 What body of land would you be on at 38°N, 22°E? _____

8 If you were on a northbound ship at 39°N, 26°E, what body of land would you probably be sailing toward?
_____

9 What island lies closest to 36°N, 28°E?
_____

10 What can be found at 38°N, 23°38′E?
_____

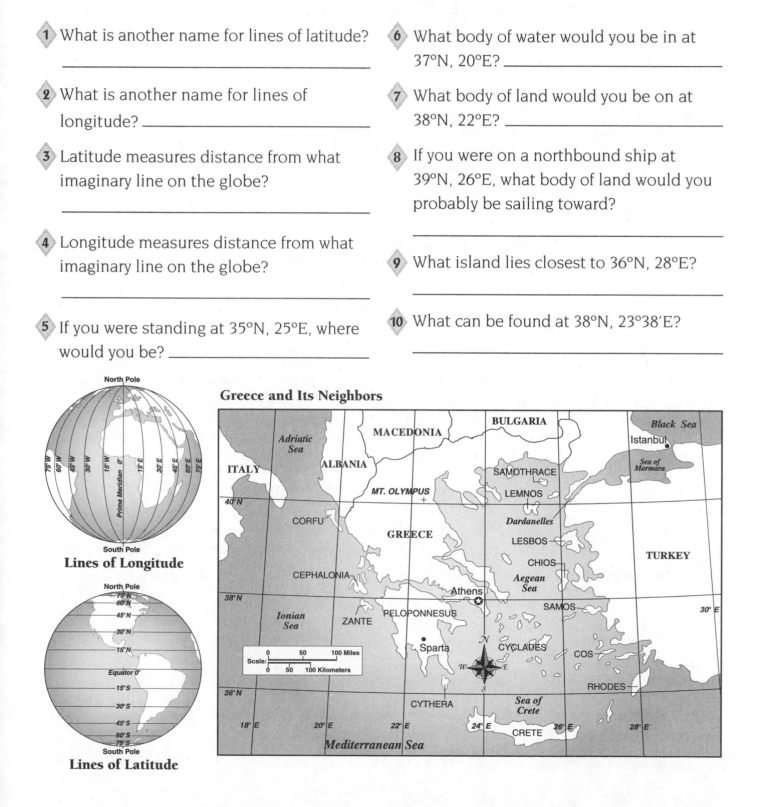

Lines of Longitude

Lines of Latitude

Greece and Its Neighbors

Getting the Lay of the Land
⤳ *Physical Geography* ⤳

Although Greece is small in size, it is made up of several kinds of landforms. This activity not only will acquaint students with Greece's geography, but it will also introduce them to a variety of different physical features.

MATERIALS

Getting the Lay of the Land (page 11)
dictionary or social studies textbook glossary
maps of modern Greece and western Turkey
[A physical map would be the most helpful, but having several different kinds of maps will make it easier for students to find the names of certain physical features.]

HERE'S HOW

1 Have students use a dictionary or social studies textbook glossary to look up the meaning of the 12 geographic terms listed on page 11. To aid your visual learners, encourage students to draw a symbol for the geographic term next to their definitions.

2 Challenge the class to use a physical map from an atlas, encyclopedia, or the Internet to find an example of each of the physical features in present-day Greece or western Turkey.

3 Finally, have students label the blank map with specific place-names of the physical features they have located (e.g., the Gulf of Messini). Since there are a number of physical features that appear repeatedly (e.g., capes and islands), you may want to invite students, individually or in groups, to find as many features as they can in a given time period. Encourage students to use multiple resources, and allow teams to divide up the work. Boost the excitement level by assigning point values to each physical feature and then have the students tally up their scores at the end of the period.

4 As a follow-up activity or as an extra challenge for students who may finish early, ask the following questions:

✻ What is the highest mountain in Greece? How tall is it? What was its significance to the ancient Greeks? (Mount Olympus; 9,570 feet; Ancient Greeks believed it was the home of the Olympian gods.)

✻ Can you find at least five of these features on a map of the United States? (Answers may vary.)

Name _____   Date _____

Getting the Lay of the Land

Imagine that you are an experienced mapmaker. It is your job to locate on the physical map below an example of each of the following landforms or physical features. Begin by finding a definition for each of these terms:

Geographic terms:

archipelago _____

bay _____

cape _____

gulf _____

isthmus _____

lake _____

mountain range _____

peninsula _____

river _____

sea _____

strait _____

valley _____

Using other maps of Greece and its neighbors, find the names of places that are examples of the 12 geographic terms listed above. Label these place-names on this map. Add the geographic term if it is not part of the name. One example has been done for you.

Physical Features: Modern Greece

CHAPTER 2

Giving Birth to History

History, Philosophy, and the Oral Tradition

During the fifth century B.C., two Greeks, Herodotus and Thucydides, invented what we think of today as historical writing. Herodotus' lively, though sometimes fanciful, account of Greece's wars with Persia earned him the nickname the "Father of History." Thucydides wrote a more serious, and more factual, record of the later wars between Athens and Sparta.

Other civilizations in the Middle East made important advances in historical writing. But the works of Herodotus and Thucydides caused a turning point in the recording of history. For the first time, writers were not trying to praise a king, pass on a religion, or honor an ancestor. Both men investigated what had happened at a given place and time, and then they recorded it—with some lapses in accuracy—for future generations.

The works of Herodotus, Thucydides, and later historians helped to preserve accounts of much of Greece's rich and turbulent past. Ancient Greek historians took it for granted that the epic poet Homer was part of that past. All ancient Greeks were raised hearing and reading tales from the blind poet's *Iliad* and *Odyssey*. However, experts today are not sure if Homer was really one poet or many. Debates also rage over whether the *Iliad* and the *Odyssey* reflect any real historic events.

Even so, the works attributed to Homer became the cornerstone of Greek society. Most Greek religious beliefs were based on the two epic poems; schoolboys were taught to read using them. Such schooling gave freeborn men like Herodotus and Thucydides a good shot at literacy. But most other social groups—women, slaves, freed slaves, and foreigners—had to rely primarily on oral communication.

Ancient literary works like the *Iliad* and the *Odyssey* were originally passed down from generation to generation by word of mouth. But word of mouth in ancient days was not what it is now in the modern era of paper and pencil. In ancient societies, it was the job of poets not only to create new works but also to preserve older compositions in their heads. In fact, poetry was used to tell stories largely because the rhymes and rhythms helped poets to better remember the words.

An experienced reciter, or storyteller, could memorize thousands of words after hearing them just once or twice. Even so, modern experts believe that ancient poets did not remember everything they heard exactly word-for-word. Instead, they caught the gist and sometimes added or subtracted passages to suit their purpose. They recited their works before large crowds, usually accompanied by music.

The oral tradition remained strong throughout the six major periods of ancient Greek history and long after. Since Europe's Renaissance, the written word has become the chief means of mass communication, and the oral tradition has declined. Along with it have gone the need and the ability to memorize long literary works after hearing them. Books and writing (and other recording devices) have done us immeasurable good, but they have also severed a link we once had with the ancient way of life.

Greeks on Greece

✑ *Primary Sources: Quotations* ✑

Ancient Greek poets, historians, and philosophers were often long winded. They spoke at length about a variety of different topics. This activity will introduce students to some of their views on life, loyalty, and the world of Greek politics. The list of quotations on pages 15 and 16 is designed to show how ancient Greeks saw themselves and their world.

MATERIALS

Greeks on Greece (pages 15 and 16)

HERE'S HOW

1 Ask students to think about what these quotes say about the Greeks. Lead a discussion about how life in ancient Greece is similar to and different from our own lives. Use each quote as a point of departure for discussions on different aspects of Greek life. For example, lead a discussion about the Plutrarch quotation on family: How many students agree? How many disagree? How would students imagine decision-making power in their future families to be handled?

VARIATIONS

◆ Select one or more quotations as a prompt for journal writing.

◆ Make a Venn diagram on the chalkboard or a large sheet of paper on which you record students' views versus ancient Greek views. Students may want to create their own diagrams on notebook paper. Discuss differences and similarities in points of view.

◆ Use the quotations as a departure point for researching specific topics. For example, students might investigate the following:

  ⁘ Who was considered a citizen in ancient Greece?

  ⁘ Greek society was divided into what social classes?

  ⁘ Who had the most power and prestige, and who had the least? (Students can develop a diagram to provide a visual format for showing the social ranking and privileges of the different groups.)

◆ Invite students to choose an ancient Greek persona (of any age, gender, or social status) and compose a response to one of the quotations based on the character's imagined experience. For example, students might write from the point of view of an Athenian woman who wants to participate in a trial, or a slave who wants to study philosophy with Socrates.

Greeks on Greece

The Gods

"The gods are near to men to watch over deeds of justice and kindliness."

—Hesiod, poet

Life in Athens

"Our constitution is called a democracy because power is in the hands not of a minority but of the whole people. . . . Here each individual is interested not only in his own affairs but in the affairs of the state as well. . . . We do not say that a man who takes no interest in politics is a man who minds his own business; we say that he has no business here at all."

—Pericles, Athenian politician

Life in Sparta

"In other cities whenever someone displays cowardice, he merely gets the name of coward; yet the coward—if he wants to—goes out in public, and sits down, and takes exercise in the same place as the brave man. But at Sparta everyone would be ashamed to be associated with a coward. . . . When sides are being picked for a ball game, that sort of man is often left out with no position assigned. And in dances he is banished to the insulting places. Moreover, in the streets he is required to give way, as well as give up his seat, even to younger men. The girls in his family he has to support at home, and he must explain to them why they cannot get husbands. He must endure having a household with no wife, and at the same time pay a fine for this."

—Xenophon, historian and soldier

Politics

"In great affairs you cannot please all parties."

—Solon, Athenian lawmaker

Family

"In a virtuous household every activity is performed by husband and wife in agreement with each other, but it is nevertheless clear that it is the man who is in charge and has the power of decision."

—Plutarch, historian and philosopher

More Life in Athens

"Future ages will wonder at us as the present age wonders at us now."

—Pericles, politician

Greeks on Greece (cont.)

Life for Girls

"Young women, in my opinion, have the sweetest existence known to mortals in their father's homes, for their innocence always keeps children safe and happy. But when [they] reach puberty and can understand, [they] are thrust out and sold away from [their] ancestral gods and from [their] parents. Some go to strange men's homes, others to foreigners', some to joyless houses, some to hostile."

—Sophocles, playwright

History

"With regard to my factual reporting of the events of the war, I have made it a principle not to write down the first story that came my way and not even to be guided by my own general impressions. Either I was present myself at the events which I have described, or else I have heard of them from eyewitnesses whose reports I have checked with as much thoroughness as possible."

—Thucydides, historian

Life for Boys

"Mother and nurse and father and tutor are vying with the other about the improvement of the child as soon as ever he is able to understand what is being said to him. . . . If he obeys, well and good; if not, he is straightened by threats and blows, like a piece of bent or warped wood."

—Protagoras, philosopher

Greeks vs. Non-Greeks

"All men, if asked to choose the best ways of ordering life, would choose their own."

—Herodotus, historian

Philosophy

"I am a lover of knowledge, and men are my teachers."

—Socrates, philosopher

Remembering Homer
~ Oral Tradition and the Iliad ~

Ever play the game "Rumor"? Well, the ancient Greeks, who were better attuned to oral discourse, could probably beat anyone alive today.

Before You Start

Be sure to read the introduction to this chapter and share information on Greek oral tradition with your students. To add an authentic flavor to this activity, encourage one of your students to dress up in Greek clothing (see pages 28 and 29) and recite the nearly 200-word passage adapted from the *Iliad* on the next page. Instruct the young actor to make his or her performance as dramatic as possible.

MATERIALS

Remembering Homer (page 19)

HERE'S HOW

1 Draw on background knowledge: Ask students if they have ever heard of the poet Homer, or of the *Iliad* or the *Odyssey*. Clarify any misconceptions and describe each poem briefly. You might show students books of the two poems to emphasize their length and the amount of text that was generated and passed on across centuries.

> ✳ Point out that these epic poems were first transmitted from one person to another at a time when few people could read or write. Ask students how they think that was possible. Discuss with them the importance of the oral tradition to ancient societies.

2 Play the game "Rumor" as a warm-up to give students a sense of the challenge of listening, remembering, and retelling information: Divide the class into four or five groups so that the students in each group are sitting or standing next to each other. Whisper William Blake's line "Tiger, Tiger burning bright/In the forests of the night" (or some other memorable phrase) to one of the students in each group. Then have that student whisper the message he or she heard to the next student, and so on, until every member of the group has heard the message. Have the last person write down what he or she heard. How close did each group get to the phrase it started off with?

3 Pass out copies of page 19, and have students read the introduction. Then read the adapted passage from the *Iliad* (next page) twice. After the first reading, ask students if there is anything about it that needs to be clarified. It may be helpful, for example, to locate Troy, the site of most of the battles between the Greeks and Trojans, and Sparta, home to King Menelaus and his wife, Helen, whose abduction by the Trojan prince Paris sparked the great war.

4 After a second reading, ask students to write down as closely as possible what they heard. Do not let them begin writing until after the passage has been read twice. Tell students that they should not try to repeat the passage word for word. Instead, they should try to get the major ideas and important phrases.

5 Finally, read the passage through again and have students compare their written version with the original. You may also want to post each student's effort on the wall along with a copy of the original passage. Who came the closest? How many details were they able to relay? How much do they think they would be able to remember tomorrow? How about next week? In Greek, this passage is rhyming poetry (the rhymes have been lost in translation). Would students have had an easier time remembering rhyme?

6 Close with a discussion that considers why people today might have more difficulty remembering the spoken word than people did in ancient times. Lead a discussion about how our communication has changed over the centuries.

The Burial of Hector, a passage adapted from Homer's *Iliad*

The people of Troy gathered around Hector's pyre just as young Dawn with her rose-red fingers shone again. They put out the last of the fires with their glistening wine, and then they collected the white bones of Hector. All his brothers and comrades mourned, with warm tears streaming down their cheeks. The bones were wrapped round and round in soft purple cloths and placed in a gold chest. The Trojans quickly lowered the chest into a deep, hollow grave, and over it they piled huge stones that were tightly packed. They then quickly heaped a mound over his grave and posted sentries for fear that the Greeks would launch an attack before the time agreed. And once they'd built the mound, they turned back home to Troy. Gathering once again, they shared a grand funeral feast in Hector's honor, held in the house of Priam, king by Zeus's will. And so they buried Hector, breaker of horses.

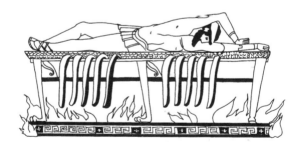

'NET LINKS

To find out more about Homer and his works, go to **http://classics.mit.edu/Homer/iliad.html** to access the text of the *Iliad* and the *Odyssey*, and go to **http://homer.reed.edu/blueseahomermap.gif** to find a map showing Homeric Greece.

Remembering Homer

Introduction

As Homer's *Iliad* begins, the Greeks have been attacking the city of Troy for ten years. The Trojans have held them off, led by the bravest of their princes, Hector. But Hector is killed by the Greek warrior Achilles. In a generous gesture, the Greeks agree to a truce so that the Trojans can mourn Hector's death. They burn Hector's body in a huge fire, called a pyre, and hold traditional ceremonies to honor the gods.

Directions

The passage you will hear from the *Iliad* describes Hector's burial. Listen carefully to the entire passage twice, then try to write down as much of it as you can remember. You're taking in this story as the ancient Greeks would have—by listening rather than reading.

_____

_____

_____

_____

_____

_____

_____

_____

_____

_____

_____

_____

_____

Mapping Greece's Past

⌐ Chronology of Historical Events ⌐ and Geographic Locations

Ancient Greece has a long history of dynamic cultural innovation and political change. By sorting out some of the more important people, places, and events, students will gain a better appreciation of the Greeks' tumultuous past.

MATERIALS

five copies of *Famous People and Events* (pages 23 and 24)
five copies of the *Famous People and Events: Ancient Greece* map (page 25)
scissors
tape or glue
textbooks and other resources (such as other nonfiction texts or Internet sites) on Greek history

HERE'S HOW

1 Label each of the five maps you copied from page 24 with one of the following headings:

Early Greece, 2000 to 800 B.C.   Hellenistic Greece, early 336 to 146 B.C.
Archaic Greece, 800 to 500 B.C.   Roman Greece, 146 B.C. to A.D. 340
Classical Greece, 500 to 300 B.C.

2 Divide the class into five groups and assign each group (or allow each group to select) a major era of Greek history from the periods listed above. Provide each group with a map of Greece, labeled appropriately, as well as a copy of *Famous People and Events* (page 23). (For large classes, you may need to divide the class into more than five groups and make extra copies of pages 23 and 24. In this case, groups may have to double up on time periods, so that two groups, for instance, may be working on Archaic Greece at the same time.)

3 Instruct each group to (a) use reference sources to find out which events on the list occurred during the era of Greek history assigned to the group; (b) determine the dates and locations of these events; and (c) complete the *Famous People and Events: Ancient Greece* map, following the directions on page 25.*

4 To make the job simpler, encourage each group to divide up the events to research among the group members.

5 After they have completed the exercise, have students choose one of the topics from their selected era and write a brief report (one or two paragraphs). Finally, have them read their reports to the rest of the class.

* Note: For most of the events listed in the exercise, students do not need to have a precise date in order to determine whether or not it belongs on their map. A few events occurred throughout the Greek-speaking world (such as the spread of ironworking) and are impossible to pinpoint. In those cases, have students place their icon somewhere on the Greek mainland (see directions, page 25).

ANSWER KEY

Famous People and Events, pages 23 and 24

Early Greece, 2000 to 800 B.C.

(7) Cretan culture begins. (Date: about 2000 B.C.; Location: Crete)

(11) Mycenaean culture begins. (Date: about 1500 B.C.; Location: Greek mainland)

(3) Dorians invade Greece and destroy Mycenaean culture. (Date: about 1200 B.C.; Location: Greek mainland)

(25) Troy is destroyed during the Trojan War. (Date: about 1184 B.C.; Location: Troy, on the west coast of modern-day Turkey)

(17) Greeks begin to colonize the Ionian coast. (Date: about 1100 B.C.; Location: western coast of modern-day Turkey)

(5) Iron becomes widely used throughout Greece. (Date: about 950 B.C.; Location: Greek mainland)

Archaic Greece, 800 to 500 B.C.

(6) The Iliad and the Odyssey are composed (centuries later, they are recorded in writing). (Date: about 800 B.C.; Location: Greek mainland)

(19) The first Olympic games are held. (Date: 776 B.C.; Location: Olympia)

(12) Greek colonies spread throughout the Mediterranean and Black seas. (Date: about 750 B.C.; Location: Mediterranean and Black seas)

(9) Spartans conquer the Messenians, enslave them, and call them "Helots." (Date: 730–710 B.C.; Location: Sparta and adjoining areas)

(30) Solon reforms Athens' laws and society. (Date: 594–593 B.C.; Location: Athens)

(10) Cleisthenes makes sweeping democratic reforms in Athens. (Date: 510 B.C.; Location: Athens)

Classical Greece, 500 to 336 B.C.

(2) Pericles is born in Athens. (Date: 490 B.C.; Location: Athens)

(16) First Persian invasion of Greece is stopped by Greek victory at Marathon. (Date: 490 B.C.; Location: Marathon, near Athens)

(22) Hippocrates, the "Father of Medicine," is born on the island of Cos, off the coast of modern-day Turkey. (Date: 460 B.C.; Location: Cos)

(14) Athens finally surrenders to Sparta after fighting two bloody wars. (Date: 404 B.C.; Location: Athens or Sparta)

(24) Socrates is executed by Athenians. (Date: 399 B.C.; Location: Athens)

(28) Sparta is defeated by Thebes and loses its status as most powerful Greek city-state. (Date: 371 B.C.; Location: Sparta or Thebes)

Hellenistic Greece, early 336 to 146 B.C.

(29) Alexander the Great of Macedonia takes power and begins conquests throughout the Mediterranean. (Date: 336 B.C.; Location: Macedonia)

(18) Aristotle founds his school of philosophy at Athens. (Date: 335 B.C.; Location: Athens)

(15) Euclid, great mathematician, opens a school and begins teaching in Alexandria, Egypt. (Date: about 300 B.C.; Location: Alexandria)

(23) Archimedes of Syracuse, a great engineer and inventor, is born. (Date: 287 B.C.; Location: Syracuse)

(26) The Colossus of Rhodes is built. (Date: 280 B.C.; Location: Rhodes)

(4) Eratosthenes, a great astronomer and mapmaker, is born in Cyrene. (Date: 276 B.C.; Location: Cyrene, in northern Africa)

Roman Greece, 146 B.C. to A.D. 340

(8) Romans conquer Greece. (Date: 147–146 B.C.; Location: Greek mainland)

(27) Romans crush Athenian revolt. (Date: 88 B.C.; Location: Athens)

(20) Plutarch, great historian, is born in Chaeronea. (Date: A.D. 47; Location: Chaeronea, near Thebes)

(1) Claudius Ptolemy, a Greek astronomer living in Alexandria, Egypt, collects and puts together extensive maps of the known world. (Date: about A.D. 150; Location: Alexandria)

(13) Romans make Byzantium their capital and rename it Constantinople. (Date: A.D. 331; Location: Constantinople, now Istanbul)

(21) Rome splits into eastern and western empires for the last time. (Date: A.D. 340; Location: Constantinople, now Istanbul)

Name _____   Date _____

Famous People and Events   Era: _____

Directions

Find the dates and locations for any of the following events which occurred during the era of Greek history written above. When your group has discovered the time and place for each event in your assigned era, create a map that highlights these events with the *Famous People and Events: Ancient Greece* map.

Date   **Location**

1. _____ _____ Claudius Ptolemy, a Greek astronomer living in Alexandria, Egypt, collects and puts together extensive maps of the known world.

2. _____ _____ Pericles is born in Athens.

3. _____ _____ Dorians invade Greece and destroy Mycenaean culture.

4. _____ _____ Eratosthenes, a great astronomer and mapmaker, is born.

5. _____ _____ Iron becomes widely used throughout Greece.

6. _____ _____ The *Iliad* and the *Odyssey* are composed (centuries later, they are recorded in writing).

7. _____ _____ Cretan culture begins.

8. _____ _____ Romans conquer Greece.

9. _____ _____ Spartans conquer the Messenians, enslave them, and call them "Helots."

10. _____ _____ Cleisthenes makes sweeping democratic reforms in Athens.

11. _____ _____ Mycenaean culture begins.

12. _____ _____ Greek colonies spread throughout the Mediterranean and Black seas.

13. _____ _____ Romans make Byzantium their capital and rename it Constantinople.

14. _____ _____ Athens finally surrenders to Sparta after fighting two bloody wars.

Famous People and Events (cont.)

Date   Location

15. _____ _____ Euclid, a great mathematician, opens a school and begins teaching.

16. _____ _____ First Persian invasion of Greece is stopped by Greek victory at Marathon.

17. _____ _____ Greeks begin to colonize the Ionian coast.

18. _____ _____ Aristotle founds his school of philosophy at Athens.

19. _____ _____ The first Olympic games are held.

20. _____ _____ Plutarch, a great historian, is born.

21. _____ _____ Rome splits into eastern and western empires for the last time.

22. _____ _____ Hippocrates, the "Father of Medicine," is born on the island of Cos.

23. _____ _____ Archimedes of Syracuse, a great engineer and inventor, is born.

24. _____ _____ Socrates is executed by Athenians.

25. _____ _____ Troy is destroyed during the Trojan War.

26. _____ _____ The Colossus of Rhodes is built.

27. _____ _____ Romans crush Athenian revolt.

28. _____ _____ Sparta is defeated by Thebes and loses its status as most powerful Greek city-state.

29. _____ _____ Alexander the Great of Macedonia takes power and begins conquests throughout the Mediterranean and into Asia Minor.

30. _____ _____ Solon reforms Athens' laws and society.

Map Key

famous person and/or event

1 ☐ _____

2 ☐ _____

3 ☐ _____

4 ☐ _____

5 ☐ _____

6 ☐ _____

☐ _____

Famous People and Events:
Ancient Greece

Era: _____

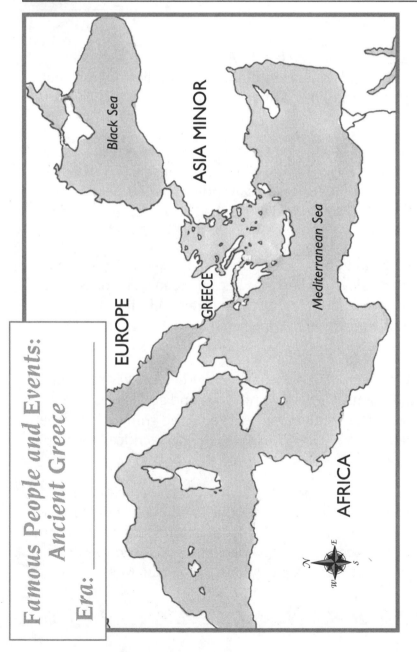

EUROPE

Black Sea

ASIA MINOR

GREECE

Mediterranean Sea

AFRICA

N E S W

Directions:

1. Label the map title above with the era of ancient Greece you have studied.

2. On the map, write in the names of the places where the six events from this era occurred. (Use the Location information from the *Famous People and Events* pages and another map to help you.)

3. Fill in the Map Key with the six events from this era: describe the six events, writing on the lines next to each box (1–6). (Use the information from the *Famous People and Events* pages to help you.)

4. In each box in the Map Key, draw an icon (a simple picture or symbol) to represent the event. For example, a spear might stand for a victory.

5. Draw each icon on the map near its correct location.

6. Use colored pencils or fine-tip markers to add color and definition to your map. For example, if you find the areas where Greeks settled during the era you researched, you might shade in these areas. (Add to the Map Key—with an explanation—any extra colors or symbols you use. This will help others better understand your map.)

CHAPTER 3

Daily Life in Ancient Greece

Clothing, Food, Games, Fables, and Religion

Many modern people see themselves as being part of a family. Ancient Greeks saw themselves as part of a household. The household included not only immediate family members, but also distant relatives, slaves, and other dependents all living under the same roof. The head of the household was the oldest male.

Men were able to leave the house and do business, exercise, gossip, and so forth. A respectable woman past the age of puberty had no such liberty. Her job was to run the household (of course, female slaves did much of the labor). Except for religious festivals, weddings, and funerals, married women were expected to stay indoors. When they did leave, they had to be accompanied by slaves or other women.

As much as 25 percent of all children born died in infancy. Those who survived—both boys and girls—spent a lot of time with their mother and slaves. When they became teenagers, boys were expected to go to school to learn rhetoric, music, and literature. Girls were taught how to spin wool and manage the household by their mothers and were considered available for marriage after their twelfth birthday. Most marriages were arranged.

There was no division between "church and state" for the ancient Greeks. Religion was such an intimate part of daily life that the Greeks did not have a word for it. Gods and goddesses were in their homes, their food, their fun, their deaths. The afterlife was believed to be grim for everyone, good or bad (though it was worse for the bad). As a result, Greeks prayed and sacrificed for help in this life, not the hereafter.

Greeks seldom did anything without first consulting the gods through seers and oracles. Seers supposedly could predict the future by looking at the innards of sacrificial animals or by observing the flight of birds. The Oracle at Delphi, sacred to Apollo, was the most prestigious oracle and famous for her tricky predictions. According to legend, one king asked if he should go to war against the Persians. The oracle replied, "You will destroy a great kingdom." So he went to war and destroyed a great kingdom—his own.

Use the activities that follow to highlight the similarities and differences between the life of ancient Greeks and our life today. How did the Greek's day-to-day lives shape their worldview—and ours?

LIBRARY LINKS

A&E/History Channel have created several entertaining videos on ancient Greek life. Look for *In Search of History: Greek Gods* at your library. It can also be ordered at **www.history.com**

'NET LINKS

The University of Pennsylvania provides one of the best overviews of daily life in ancient Greece: **http://www.museum.upenn.edu/Greek_World/Index.html**

Fifth Century B.C. Fashion
~ Ancient Greek Clothing ~

The *chiton* (KY-ton) was one of the most popular—but by no means the only—form of Greek dress for both men and women. A chiton was usually made of wool, but a cotton sheet will do for your students.

MATERIALS

Greek Fashion: Fifth Century B.C. (page 29)
measuring tape
large pieces of fabric, such as old bedsheets (see measurement information below)
safety pins (about 5–8 per student)
thin strips of fabric (about 3 feet long) or belts
scissors
needle and thread (optional)
brooches (optional)

HERE'S HOW

1 Have students each bring in (or ask for donations of) large pieces of fabric, such as bedsheets.*

2 Show some models of ancient Greek dress from around the 5th century B.C.

3 Ask students to comment on the types of clothing ancient Greeks wore. Does the chiton look comfortable? Practical? Discuss why Greeks might have worn such an outfit. What practical purposes did it serve? How would it have been useful for doing manual labor? Would it have helped them cope with the warm Greek climate? Students may notice that chitons were worn by both men and women and differed in length. Men might also have draped a rectangular cloth, called a *himation*, over their shoulders for decorative emphasis.

4 Distribute copies of *Greek Fashion: Fifth Century* B.C. and walk students through the steps of constructing a chiton. (You may want to model constructing one with a student volunteer first.) When students make their chitons, it will be easiest for them to measure and fasten materials in pairs.

5 Use the chitons when your students give oral reports or presentations on ancient Greek subjects, perform *Antigone* (pages 47–54), and enact the trial from *Murder in Athens* (pages 71–79).

*Note: Most bed sheets will not provide enough material to make an authentic chiton. If your class is using bedsheets, simply make the width of the chiton (Measurement A on page 27) equal to the length of the sheet. This variation will still provide plenty of material for a good-looking garment.

'NET LINKS
Check out the following Web site to see how the ancient Greeks dressed:
http://www.firstnethou.com/annam/costhist.html/ancient.html/index.html

Greek Fashion: Fifth Century B.C.

Here's how to make a *chiton* (KY-ton) and look like an ancient Greek:

1 Stretch your arms out so that they are straight and level with your shoulders (see the illustration below). Have a partner measure the length between your fingertips (Measurement A). For girls, have your partner measure the length from your ankle to the base of your neck (Measurement B). For boys, have your partner measure from your kneecap to the base of your neck (Measurement B).

2 Your piece of cloth should be twice as wide as Measurement A. So if you are 36 inches from fingertip to fingertip, the cloth should be twice as wide, or 72 inches. However, *do not* double Measurement B. If you are 45 inches from neck to ankles (or kneecaps), make sure the cloth is exactly that long. Trim the material as necessary.

3 Fold the cloth over so that it matches Measurement A. Pin or sew up the length of the chiton. You should end up with a tube of cloth that reaches from fingertip to fingertip and from your neck to your ankles (for girls) or kneecaps (for boys).

4 Step inside the tube and lift the garment up to your shoulders. At the top opening, use pins or brooches at four or five places to form a neckline and loose sleeves, leaving plenty of room for your head and arms to poke through.

5 Now that you've secured the chiton, tie a strip of fabric or put a belt around the waist. Pull the excess part up over the belt.

Measurement A

Measurement B

pin or sew together the open ends

fasten cloth

If you want to accessorize, girls can try gold earrings and bracelets and decorative hair bands, while boys can try a brimless cap, called a *pilos*, or a long rectangular piece of fabric worn over both shoulders (or over one shoulder to leave the fighting arm free), called a *himation*.

Greek Treats
ᔕ Ancient Greek Cuisine ᔕ

Tastes have changed since the times of ancient Greece. Somebody holding a fancy dinner party in Greece during the 3rd century B.C. might have served up fried grasshoppers as an appetizer. The recipe is easy: Put the (presumably live) grasshoppers in a covered pan coated with olive oil and lightly brown them.

Whether they were eating grasshoppers or not, Greeks knew how to live it up at a meal. A large feast, called a symposium, was a great chance for men—and only men—to get together to talk, drink wine, and eat delicacies, such as eel. But the day-to-day Greek diet was pretty monotonous by modern standards, made up primarily of bread and supplemented mostly by fruits and vegetables. Meat was rarely eaten, except at religious festivals, though fish was fairly common. Figs, nuts, and olives were plentiful. Olive oil was a staple cooking ingredient for almost any meal.

MATERIALS

Greek Treats (page 31)

HERE'S HOW

1 Have students make a list of the types of food they ate for dinner within the last week. See if they can identify any patterns among their choices of food. They should be able to identify common foods that most students in class eat.

2 List on the board some of the following ingredients ancient Greeks would have had available to them: eggs; olives; figs; nuts; grapes; apples; pears; cheese and milk (sheep and goat products); salt; olive oil; vinegar; fish (including eel and anchovies); pork; honey; barley; wheat (imported from other countries); and wild herbs and spices, such as garlic, leeks, dill, and fennel. Discuss what kinds of dishes students can imagine making from these ingredients.

3 Remind the class that modern food preparation and storage techniques would not have been used. To store food, fruits were often dried, and meats and fish were often salted or pickled.

4 If possible, in class prepare some of the traditional Greek recipes found in *Greek Treats* (note that these are not "ancient" recipes, but some elements of preparation and/or ingredients may have been passed down from ancient times). Distribute copies of page 31 so that students can become familiar with all the necessary ingredients. If you cannot prepare the recipes in class, ask student volunteers to make a dish at home under adult supervision. After sampling the results, discuss how these dishes compare with most modern foods.

5 Discuss the staple diet of the Greeks and compare it with students' diets.

LIBRARY LINKS

Food and Feasts in Ancient Greece by Imogen Dawson provides the best introduction to Greek cuisine and dining. It is nicely illustrated and is written for young teenagers.

Greek Treats

Imagine that you are a world-class chef. Try preparing the following traditional Greek recipes. Today these foods are enjoyed all around the world.

Yogurt With Honey and Almonds

Ingredients	Materials
1/4 cup chopped almonds	measuring cup
1/4 cup honey	mixing bowl
2 1/2 cups yogurt	large spoon

Directions

1 Measure ingredients and put them in mixing bowl.

2 Stir them until well mixed and leave for 10 minutes.

~ THE ~
SPARTAN WAY

The Spartans, who delighted in doing things the hard way, made their staple food a famously bad dish called "black broth." The exact recipe is lost to history. But the ingredients to this wicked-tasting stuff supposedly included pork (including fat), vinegar, and salt. Spartans enjoyed watching visitors taste it and spit it out.

Stuffed Fig Leaves

Ingredients	Materials
1 to 2 dozen fig leaves	mixing bowl
1 1/2 cups flour	large sauce pan
1/4 teaspoon salt	teaspoon
4 tablespoons shortening	tablespoon
2 eggs	measuring cup
1/4 cup milk	a clean work surface
1 tablespoon honey	glass dish with a cover or aluminum foil
1/2 cup Parmesan cheese	

Directions

1 Mix flour, salt, and shortening. Then add the remaining ingredients (except for the fig leaves) until they form a dough.

2 Boil water in the saucepan. Put fig leaves into boiling water for about one minute and then remove.

3 Lay out the fig leaves on a clean surface. Put a tablespoon of dough at the stem end of the fig leaves and roll them up, tucking in the sides as you go.

4 Place stuffed leaves in covered glass dish, pour in a cup of hot water, and let simmer in the oven for 30 to 40 minutes at 300°F.

Dog Eat Dog: Polis Board Game

Ancient Greek Games

Polis was the word that Greeks used for their main unit of government. But it was also the name of a popular board game that was similar to chess. (It frequently went by the name *Petteia*, or pebbles.) The 16 pieces used to play the game were called "dogs." The rules that have been passed down to us from both Greek and Roman authors are sketchy and may be incomplete. However, given what we know, it is possible to construct a challenging board game. Similar games are still played in North Africa and Asia.

Background

The polis, or city-state, was the basic political unit of ancient Greece, the way countries are for us today. We are not sure of the origins of the names of this game and its pieces. At least one historian has speculated that the game's name comes from the way Greeks fought. A group of armored hoplites, or soldiers, from the same polis would march into battle in lockstep. Their Greek enemies marched out to meet them in the same way. Each soldier's polis made him strong and secure. Without the mutual support of the polis, an individual would be defenseless.

MATERIALS

Polis Game Board (page 34)—one copy per pair of players,
8 pennies and 8 nickels to serve as opposing "dogs" (you can also use buttons, bottle caps, pebbles, or other small objects, as long as each pair of players has 8 of one type and 8 of another)

HERE'S HOW

1 Discuss the importance of the polis to the ancient Greeks and the theory behind the name of this interesting board game.

2 Divide your class into pairs, pass out a set of materials to each twosome, and review the rules of the game. As part of your discussion, draw on the board the five grids shown on the next page. These should help the class better understand the rules.

3 After the students have enjoyed playing a game or two, discuss some strategy moves they learned after playing several rounds. Like chess, this strategy game teaches kids to think critically, problem-solve, and plan ahead.

> ### LIBRARY LINKS
> An out-of-print book titled *A History of Board Games Other Than Chess*, by H.J.R. Murray, provides a great introduction to the board games of ancient civilizations.

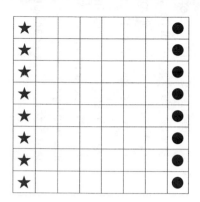

Rule 1: Each side lines up its dogs along opposite sides of the game board.

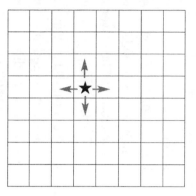

Rule 2: On a turn, a player may move his or her dog an unlimited number of spaces in any direction (except diagonally). A player must stop moving when his or her dog is blocked by any other dog.

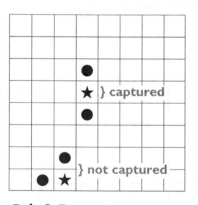

Rule 3: To capture an opponent's dog, a player must surround the opponent's dog on two sides. A player can surround an opponent's dog either in the front and back or on both sides, but not diagonally. In this example, two circles have captured a star. The circles below, however, have not captured the star.

Rule 4: To capture two or more of an opponent's dogs at once, a player must surround a line of his or her opponent's dogs at both ends. Two stars are captured in this example.

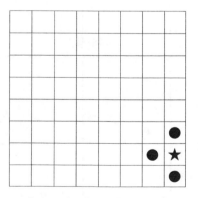

Rule 5: The first player to take all of his or her opponent's dogs wins. A player may also win by cornering his or her opponent's remaining dogs so they cannot move, as shown above: The star is cornered and defeated.

Polis Game Board

The ancient Greeks loved to play games. After reading the rules below, try playing a game or two of Polis with a partner.

Rules

1. Each side lines up its dogs along opposite sides of the game board. The player with the smaller dogs goes first.

2. On a turn, you may move your dog an unlimited number of spaces in any direction, except diagonally (like a rook in chess). You must stop moving when your dog is blocked by any other dog.

3. To capture an opponent's dog, you must surround it on two sides. You can surround your opponent's dog either in the front and back or on both sides, but not diagonally.

4. To capture two or more of your opponent's dogs at once, you must surround a line of your opponent's dogs at both ends.

5. You win the game by taking all of your opponent's dogs. You can also win by blocking your opponent's dogs so they cannot move.

Aesop's Fables

⤳ The Origin and Structure of Fables ⤳

Aesop is the best known of all fable-tellers, but we know very little about his life. He is believed to have been a Greek slave who lived around the middle of the 6th century B.C. After Aesop died, newly created fables were attributed to him, so it is not clear how many of "Aesop's fables" Aesop actually composed. What we do know is that the fable—a brief story that teaches something—remains a great way to impart ethical lessons. The original fables did not have a moral attached to the end since a good fable has many interpretations. However, it has become traditional to state the moral at the end of each fable.

MATERIALS

Unfinished Fables (page 37)
lined paper

HERE'S HOW

1 Explain who Aesop was and describe a fable. Then read the first fable, below, including the moral at the end, as an example.

2 Read the next three fables without reading the accompanying morals. After you read each one, have students suggest their own morals. Write their suggestions on the chalkboard. How do their morals compare to the one traditionally given?

3 Pass out copies of page 37. Explain to students that they will complete each modern-day fable in their own words. They can write as much or as little as they want. Encourage them to be as funny and original as possible. However, their fable must have a point, and they should be able to explain its moral.

4 Invite students to come up with their own fables. Aesop often used animals as his main characters because they were familiar to ancient Greeks. However, students should feel free to use modern objects, such as cars and TVs. They should also try to give the fable a "twist," so that the ending is unexpected. Again, the fable can be long or short, but either way it should have a clear point that students can explain.

Aesop's Fables

I. There was a shepherd who was fond of playing practical jokes. He would drive his flock some distance from the village and then shout to his neighbors for help, saying that wolves had attacked his sheep. Two or three times the townsfolk came rushing out in alarm—and then returned home with the shepherd laughing at them, for there was no wolf. Eventually, however, some wolves actually came and threatened the man's flock. The shepherd called to his neighbors for help, but they thought he was up to his usual tricks and did not respond. The shepherd lost all of his sheep.

Moral: People quickly disbelieve somebody who raises false alarms.

II. On a hot, thirsty summer's day, a lion and a boar came to drink at a small spring. They started quarreling over which one would take the first drink. Pretty soon they were both fighting for their lives. But stopping for a moment to take a breath, they looked around and saw some vultures waiting to eat the loser of their battle. That made them stop fighting. "It is better for us to be friends," they said, "than to be eaten by vultures and crows."

Moral: Bitterness and fighting cause danger for those who don't have the sense to get along.

III. A fox poked fun at a lioness because she had only one lion cub. "Only one," she replied, "but a lion."

Moral: It is quality, not quantity, that counts.

IV. A tortoise asked an eagle to teach it to fly. The eagle pointed out that tortoises do not have the proper bodies for flying. But the tortoise was determined and kept asking. So the eagle took the tortoise in his talons, flew up very high, and let the tortoise go. The tortoise fell on some rocks and was killed.

Moral: Sometimes envy makes people disregard wise advice.

'NET LINKS

Art students at the University of Massachusetts at Amherst created charming "traditional" and "modern" illustrations for Aesop's fables: **http://www.umass.edu/aesop/**

Unfinished Fables

Below are some partially written modern fables. Finish each one and include your own moral at the end. (Hint: If you're having trouble getting started, you might begin with the moral and then finish the story in a way that fits your moral.)

1. One day, a computer said to a mouse pad, "You are nothing without me! I have all the circuits, all the software. I am the reason that you exist." "Ah," said the mouse pad, "but . . .

_____

_____

_____

_____

Moral: _____

_____

2. Three bees were hovering around a flower one spring day when a woman walked by. The first bee flew away in fear. The second bee, believing that the woman did not notice him, decided to sit still and see what happened. The third bee . . .

_____

_____

_____

_____

Moral: _____

_____

3. One day an auto mechanic was working on a car that had broken down. The mechanic was puzzled because he could not figure out what the problem was. He tried everything he knew, and still the car would not run. Finally, he threw up his arms in frustration, saying to the car, "How do I make you work again?" The car replied . . .

_____

_____

_____

_____

Moral: _____

_____

Gods and Goddesses
☙ *Ancient Greek Religion* ☙

This exercise is designed to acquaint your students with some of the gods and goddesses worshipped by the ancient Greeks.

MATERIALS

Gods and Goddesses (page 39)
Gods and Goddesses Flash Cards (pages 40–44)

scissors
tape or glue

HERE'S HOW

1 Familiarize your students with the role of gods and goddesses in the daily life of ancient Greece; see *Daily Life in Ancient Greece* on page 26.

2 Make a class set of copies of page 39. You will need to make enough copies of pages 40–44 so that each student or pair of students can have a set of cards. Copying these flash cards onto thicker paper or card stock will make them more durable. [Tip: When the cards have been assembled, laminate them to create a permanent set.]

3 Distribute the sets of flash card pages to your students and have them cut out the cards. To assemble each card, students should fold along the middle line and either tape or glue the two sides of the cards together.

4 Allow time for the class to study the characteristics of each god. Here are three suggestions:

✳ Have students look at the name side and then turn the card over to discover the attributes each god possesses. Then have them reverse the process, looking at the attributes and trying to guess the god's name.

✳ Play a game of 20 Questions in which you or a student select a god or goddess and have students ask yes-or-no questions (about gender, powers, duties, weapons, and so on) to figure out the identity of the chosen deity.

✳ Create a family-tree mural on a bulletin board to show the relationships among the gods and goddesses. Have each student or pair of students contribute a drawing of a god or goddess to the class mural. (You may need to model the symbols and organization for a family tree first.)

5 Once students are familiar with the names and attributes of the gods and goddesses, distribute page 38 and challenge students to answer the questions without referring to the flash cards. Cut off the answer box at the bottom to make the assignment more challenging.

6 Finally, lead a discussion about the Greek gods. What does the class think of the Olympians' behavior? How do ancient Greek ideas about religion differ from modern views?

ANSWER KEY Gods and Goddesses (page 38) 1. Poseidon; 2. Aphrodite; 3. Hera; 4. Ares; 5. Demeter; 6. Hestia; 7. Athena; 8. Hephaestus; 9. Artemis; 10. Brothers; Bonus question: Cronus and Rhea

Name _____   Date _____

Gods and Goddesses

Study the information on your flash cards and then answer the questions below.

1 Greek sailors in a storm-tossed ship probably would have prayed to _____ .

2 The goddess of love was _____ .

3 _____ had a stormy marriage with Zeus.

4 Before battle, a soldier would probably have prayed to _____ .

5 Farmers at harvest time would have prayed to _____ .

6 Orphans and homeless children prayed to _____ for help.

7 Philosophers prayed to _____ for wisdom.

8 Blacksmiths prayed to _____ for greater skill.

9 Hunters who killed more than they could eat were believed to be punished by

_____ .

10 Zeus and Hades are related to each other as _____ .

Bonus question

_____ and _____ were Titans and were
the parents of many Olympian gods.

- -

Answer Box

 Athena	 Cronus and Rhea	 Aphrodite	 Demeter	 Poseidon
 Artemis	 Hera	 Hestia	 Hephaestus	 Ares

Gods and Goddesses Flash Cards

Cut along the dotted lines (- - -). Fold along the solid line (———).

Zeus
(zoos)

Parents: Cronus (CROH-nus) and Rhea (REE-uh)

Married to: Hera

Home: Mount Olympus

Title: All-powerful king of the gods, with special duties as god of the sky.

Weapon of Choice: Thunderbolt and lightning

Sacred Symbols: Oak tree and eagle

Powers: Punishing crime, avenging wrong, protecting faithful worshippers, and controlling all good and evil with justice

Pastimes: Breaking up fights between other gods, bickering with his wife, and wooing mortal women and goddesses

Background: He was a superior leader of the Olympian gods. He helped them to win a long, fierce war over the Titan gods, who were the Olympians' parents and relatives.

Hera
(HEER-uh)

Parents: Cronus (CROH-nus) and Rhea (REE-uh)

Married to: Zeus

Home: Mount Olympus

Title: Queen of the gods; also goddess of women and motherhood

Weapon of Choice: Prophesy and trickery

Sacred Symbols: None

Powers: Commanding the winds and watching over women and mothers

Pastimes: Punishing the women wooed by Zeus (as well as their children), plotting against Zeus, and helping her favorite mortals

Background: This goddess feuded with her unfaithful husband, Zeus. She liked to favor certain mortals and helped them behind Zeus's back. He generally disapproved of such favoritism.

Poseidon
(poh-SY-duhn)

Parents: Cronus (CROH-nus) and Rhea (REE-uh)

Married to: Amphitrite (am-fih-TRY-tee), a minor goddess

Home: Mount Olympus and all the waters of the earth

Title: God of the seas and navigation

Weapon of Choice: Trident (could cause storms, floods, and earthquakes to occur; springs to flow; and rivers to dry up)

Sacred Symbols: Pine tree and horse

Powers: Causing or calming earthquakes, storms, and other natural disasters

Pastimes: Inventing animals such as the horse and dolphin, feuding with Athena over control of Athens, and extending his domain with floods and storms.

Background: This god was moody and jealous of his more powerful brother, Zeus, chief god. He could reward a coastal city for decades with calm seas, favorable winds, and plentiful fishing. Then, for no reason, he would hurl a hurricane at it.

Gods and Goddesses Flash Cards

Cut along the dotted lines (- - -). Fold along the solid line (——).

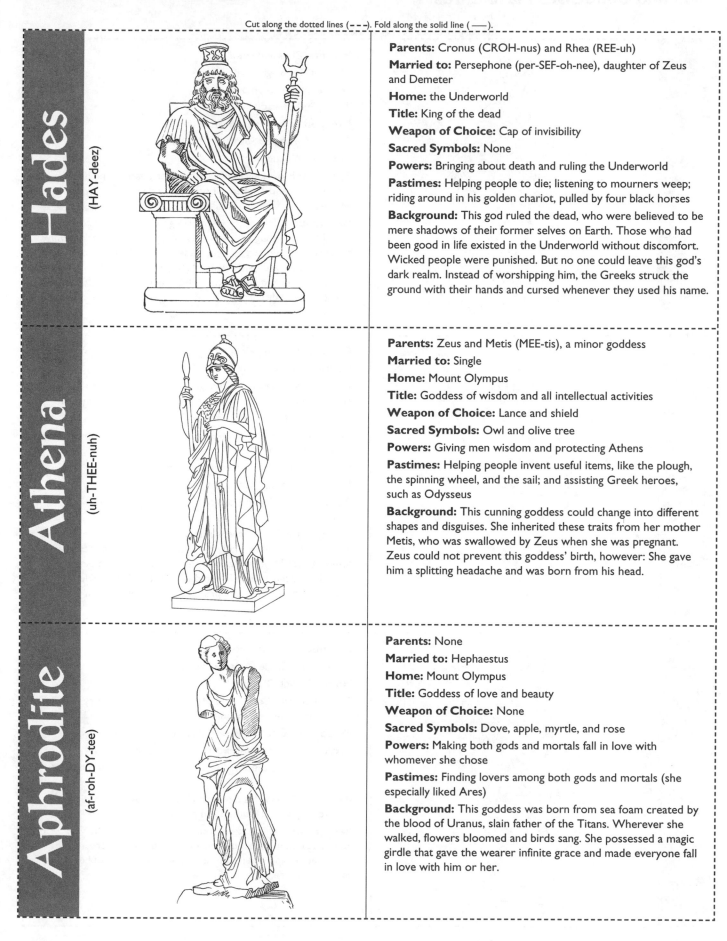

Hades (HAY-deez)

Parents: Cronus (CROH-nus) and Rhea (REE-uh)

Married to: Persephone (per-SEF-oh-nee), daughter of Zeus and Demeter

Home: the Underworld

Title: King of the dead

Weapon of Choice: Cap of invisibility

Sacred Symbols: None

Powers: Bringing about death and ruling the Underworld

Pastimes: Helping people to die; listening to mourners weep; riding around in his golden chariot, pulled by four black horses

Background: This god ruled the dead, who were believed to be mere shadows of their former selves on Earth. Those who had been good in life existed in the Underworld without discomfort. Wicked people were punished. But no one could leave this god's dark realm. Instead of worshipping him, the Greeks struck the ground with their hands and cursed whenever they used his name.

Athena (uh-THEE-nuh)

Parents: Zeus and Metis (MEE-tis), a minor goddess

Married to: Single

Home: Mount Olympus

Title: Goddess of wisdom and all intellectual activities

Weapon of Choice: Lance and shield

Sacred Symbols: Owl and olive tree

Powers: Giving men wisdom and protecting Athens

Pastimes: Helping people invent useful items, like the plough, the spinning wheel, and the sail; and assisting Greek heroes, such as Odysseus

Background: This cunning goddess could change into different shapes and disguises. She inherited these traits from her mother Metis, who was swallowed by Zeus when she was pregnant. Zeus could not prevent this goddess' birth, however: She gave him a splitting headache and was born from his head.

Aphrodite (af-roh-DY-tee)

Parents: None

Married to: Hephaestus

Home: Mount Olympus

Title: Goddess of love and beauty

Weapon of Choice: None

Sacred Symbols: Dove, apple, myrtle, and rose

Powers: Making both gods and mortals fall in love with whomever she chose

Pastimes: Finding lovers among both gods and mortals (she especially liked Ares)

Background: This goddess was born from sea foam created by the blood of Uranus, slain father of the Titans. Wherever she walked, flowers bloomed and birds sang. She possessed a magic girdle that gave the wearer infinite grace and made everyone fall in love with him or her.

Gods and Goddesses Flash Cards

Cut along the dotted lines (– – –). Fold along the solid line (——).

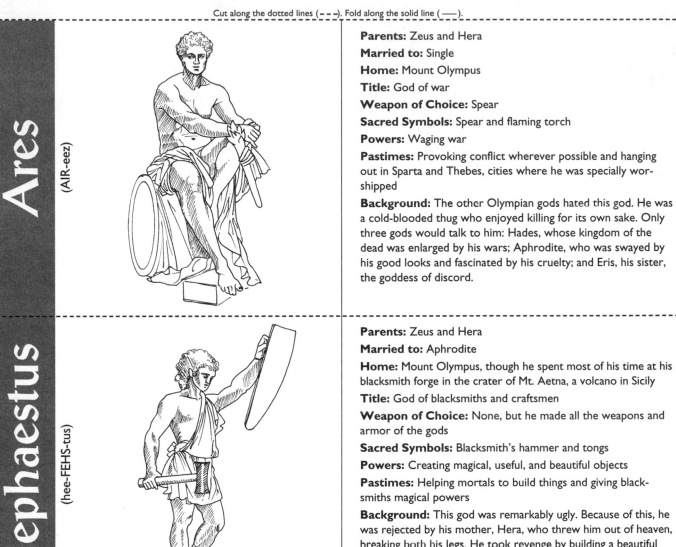

Ares
(AIR-eez)

Parents: Zeus and Hera

Married to: Single

Home: Mount Olympus

Title: God of war

Weapon of Choice: Spear

Sacred Symbols: Spear and flaming torch

Powers: Waging war

Pastimes: Provoking conflict wherever possible and hanging out in Sparta and Thebes, cities where he was specially worshipped

Background: The other Olympian gods hated this god. He was a cold-blooded thug who enjoyed killing for its own sake. Only three gods would talk to him: Hades, whose kingdom of the dead was enlarged by his wars; Aphrodite, who was swayed by his good looks and fascinated by his cruelty; and Eris, his sister, the goddess of discord.

Hephaestus
(hee-FEHS-tus)

Parents: Zeus and Hera

Married to: Aphrodite

Home: Mount Olympus, though he spent most of his time at his blacksmith forge in the crater of Mt. Aetna, a volcano in Sicily

Title: God of blacksmiths and craftsmen

Weapon of Choice: None, but he made all the weapons and armor of the gods

Sacred Symbols: Blacksmith's hammer and tongs

Powers: Creating magical, useful, and beautiful objects

Pastimes: Helping mortals to build things and giving blacksmiths magical powers

Background: This god was remarkably ugly. Because of this, he was rejected by his mother, Hera, who threw him out of heaven, breaking both his legs. He took revenge by building a beautiful chair that closed around her and wouldn't let her go. He finally released her only after she promised to accept him as a god.

Apollo
(uh-PAH-loh)

Parents: Zeus and Leto (LEE-toh), a minor goddess

Married to: Single (Artemis' twin)

Home: Mount Olympus

Title: Sun god; also the god of medicine, music, poetry, dance, mathematics, herdsmen, and prophecy

Weapon of Choice: Bow and arrow

Sacred Symbols: Laurel tree and the number seven

Powers: Making the sun rise, promoting learning, and healing people

Pastimes: Driving his fiery sun chariot across the daytime sky and wooing mortal women and goddesses

Background: This god embodied the Greek ideal: he was young, beautiful, wise, just, and moderate. He also created the Oracle at Delphi, where a priestess would make prophecies about the future.

Gods and Goddesses Flash Cards

Cut along the dotted lines (- - -). Fold along the solid line (——).

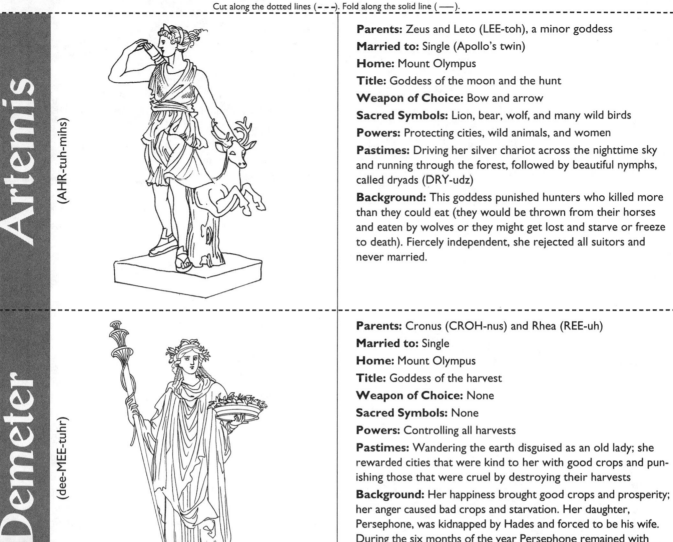

Artemis
(AHR-tuh-mihs)

Parents: Zeus and Leto (LEE-toh), a minor goddess

Married to: Single (Apollo's twin)

Home: Mount Olympus

Title: Goddess of the moon and the hunt

Weapon of Choice: Bow and arrow

Sacred Symbols: Lion, bear, wolf, and many wild birds

Powers: Protecting cities, wild animals, and women

Pastimes: Driving her silver chariot across the nighttime sky and running through the forest, followed by beautiful nymphs, called dryads (DRY-udz)

Background: This goddess punished hunters who killed more than they could eat (they would be thrown from their horses and eaten by wolves or they might get lost and starve or freeze to death). Fiercely independent, she rejected all suitors and never married.

Demeter
(dee-MEE-tuhr)

Parents: Cronus (CROH-nus) and Rhea (REE-uh)

Married to: Single

Home: Mount Olympus

Title: Goddess of the harvest

Weapon of Choice: None

Sacred Symbols: None

Powers: Controlling all harvests

Pastimes: Wandering the earth disguised as an old lady; she rewarded cities that were kind to her with good crops and punishing those that were cruel by destroying their harvests

Background: Her happiness brought good crops and prosperity; her anger caused bad crops and starvation. Her daughter, Persephone, was kidnapped by Hades and forced to be his wife. During the six months of the year Persephone remained with him, this goddess made the earth barren. During the six months Persephone visited her mother, the Earth blossomed again.

Hermes
(HER-meez)

Parents: Zeus and Maia (MY-uh), a minor goddess

Married to: Single

Home: Mount Olympus

Title: Messenger of gods; also, god of dreams, commerce, treaties, travelers, inventions, science, arts, and oratory

Weapon of Choice: None (he carried a messenger's staff with a white ribbon that marked him as neutral in any conflict)

Sacred Symbols: The number four

Powers: Traveling anywhere instantly

Pastimes: Delivering messages for the gods and escorting all dead people to the Underworld

Background: This witty and cunning god invented sandals as well as a new musical instrument, the lyre. He also stole a herd of cattle from his half-brother, Apollo.

Gods and Goddesses Flash Cards

Cut along the dotted lines (– – –). Fold along the solid line (——).

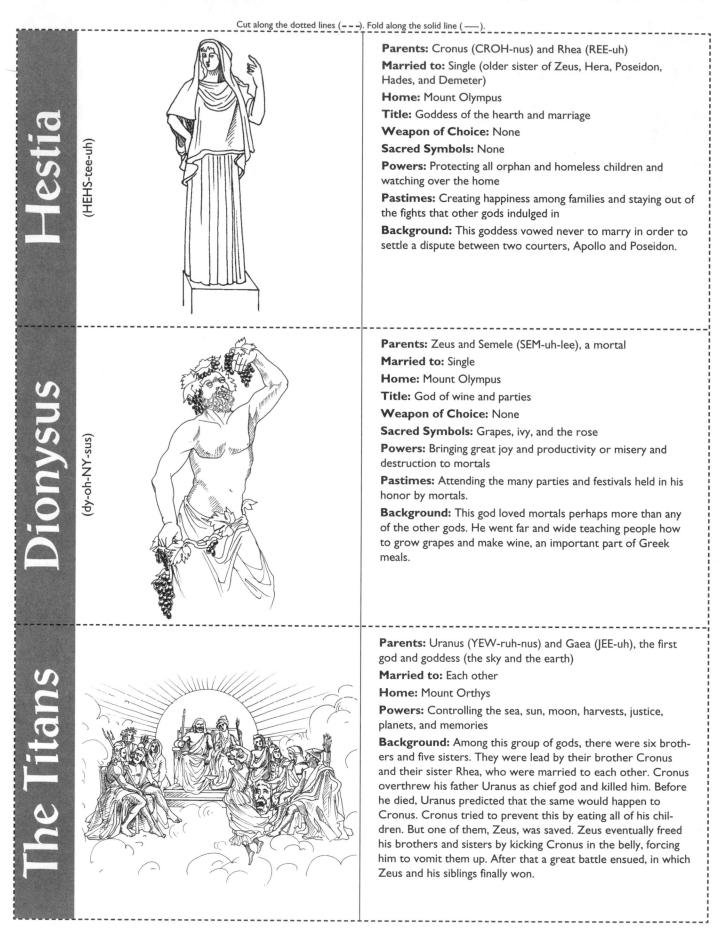

Hestia
(HEHS-tee-uh)

Parents: Cronus (CROH-nus) and Rhea (REE-uh)

Married to: Single (older sister of Zeus, Hera, Poseidon, Hades, and Demeter)

Home: Mount Olympus

Title: Goddess of the hearth and marriage

Weapon of Choice: None

Sacred Symbols: None

Powers: Protecting all orphan and homeless children and watching over the home

Pastimes: Creating happiness among families and staying out of the fights that other gods indulged in

Background: This goddess vowed never to marry in order to settle a dispute between two courters, Apollo and Poseidon.

Dionysus
(dy-oh-NY-sus)

Parents: Zeus and Semele (SEM-uh-lee), a mortal

Married to: Single

Home: Mount Olympus

Title: God of wine and parties

Weapon of Choice: None

Sacred Symbols: Grapes, ivy, and the rose

Powers: Bringing great joy and productivity or misery and destruction to mortals

Pastimes: Attending the many parties and festivals held in his honor by mortals.

Background: This god loved mortals perhaps more than any of the other gods. He went far and wide teaching people how to grow grapes and make wine, an important part of Greek meals.

The Titans

Parents: Uranus (YEW-ruh-nus) and Gaea (JEE-uh), the first god and goddess (the sky and the earth)

Married to: Each other

Home: Mount Orthys

Powers: Controlling the sea, sun, moon, harvests, justice, planets, and memories

Background: Among this group of gods, there were six brothers and five sisters. They were lead by their brother Cronus and their sister Rhea, who were married to each other. Cronus overthrew his father Uranus as chief god and killed him. Before he died, Uranus predicted that the same would happen to Cronus. Cronus tried to prevent this by eating all of his children. But one of them, Zeus, was saved. Zeus eventually freed his brothers and sisters by kicking Cronus in the belly, forcing him to vomit them up. After that a great battle ensued, in which Zeus and his siblings finally won.

CHAPTER 4

A Closer Look:
Greek Language, Art, and Science

Vocabulary, Drama, Art and Architecture, and Science

It is impossible to calculate the impact of ancient Greece on modern learning, art, and science. The lengthy list of English words on page 46 should provide you with a rough idea of the large number of Greek words and ideas we have adopted.

Theater, for instance, is both a word and concept derived from the vocabulary of the ancient Athenians, who took drama very seriously. The historian Plutarch said that they spent more on their dramatic performances than they did on their entire defense budget. Prisoners were often let out on bail so they could attend plays.

However, the Greeks handled theater much differently than we do today. Plays were put on only twice a year at festivals honoring the god Dionysus. Each play was shown only once and then never acted out again. (In the 4th century B.C. many favorite plays were finally revived.) Spectators often sat through an entire day of shows, usually at least four plays. When the audience became cranky and bored, they vented their frustration by pelting the actors (always men) with rocks and fruit.

The Greeks became famous not only for the plays that make great theater, but also for the theaters where great plays were staged. Their genius for architecture and artistic decoration is the most visible reminder of their legacy. Few modern buildings completely escape the influence of the Greeks, and in ancient times, almost none did. Instead, kings and rulers around the Mediterranean vied to build the biggest structures they could afford with the help of Greek architects, artisans, and engineers. A handful of those structures became part of what is known today as the Seven Wonders of the Ancient World.

All the great Greek wonders today lie in ruins or have disappeared. Unfortunately, a lot of ancient Greek learning and philosophy is in similar shape. We possess only fragments from the philosophical writings that came before Plato and Aristotle. Philosophers in ancient Greece pondered weighty matters, but they were also practical scientists and mathematicians. One of the greatest of them was Pythagoras, whose famous theorem is one of geometry's fundamental concepts.

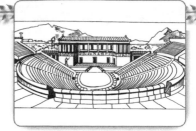

It's All Greek to Me
~ Word Origins ~

All of the common English words below are taken from vocabulary and concepts that were originally Greek. In some cases, such as "athlete," the ancient Greeks simply gave a name to an everyday person, place, or thing. But in other cases, such as "atom" and "drama," they invented the idea that goes with the word.

MATERIALS

paper
list of words, below
dictionary that provides etymology (word origins)

HERE'S HOW

1 Divide your class into groups and assign each one a few words from the list below.

2 Ask students to use a dictionary to look up the modern definition of each word. The dictionary will indicate its Greek root and explain whether the ancient Greeks had a different definition for that word.

3 Where it is applicable, have students write out the definition of the Greek word (or its root) and compare it to the modern meaning. Dividing their paper into a t-chart with the categories "Greek meaning" and "Modern meaning" can help students graphically compare the different meanings. Visual learners may benefit from drawing

	Greek Meaning	Modern Meaning
school		
academy		
geometry		

cartoons of contrasting meanings in the margins, next to the definitions (note that drawing may not lend itself to the more abstract definitions). Then lead the class in a discussion about the ways in which words change meaning over time.

ΣΔΩΣΔΩΣΔΩΣΔΩΣΔΩΣΔΩΣΔΩΣΔΩΣΔΩΣΔΩΣΔΩΣΔΩΣΔΩΣΔΩΣΔΩ

school	melody	metropolis
academy	harmony	democracy
geometry	symphony	aristocracy
physics	chorus	monarchy
atom	theater	despot
philosophy	drama	tyrant
astronomy	comedy	ostracism
star	tragedy	athlete
galaxy	critic	gymnasium
comet	history	stadium
poet	politics	architect
music		

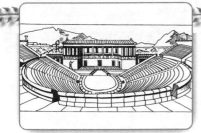

Antigone

⤳ Ancient Greek Tragedy ⤳

This play, the action of which follows Sophocles' *Oedipus the King* and *Oedipus at Colonus*, revolves around a conflict between two characters named Antigone and Creon. Antigone is the daughter of Oedipus, the former ruler of Thebes. In *Oedipus the King*, Oedipus discovers that he has unknowingly killed his father and married his mother, Jocasta. Oedipus blinds himself in grief and shame and flees the city. Jocasta kills herself.

Antigone has two brothers, Polynices and Eteocles, and a sister named Ismene. After Oedipus leaves Thebes in disgrace, Polynices and Eteocles share power. The two quarrel, however, and Polynices leaves. He returns with an army intent on taking and destroying Thebes. Eteocles defends the city, and in the battle that follows, the two brothers kill each other. Polynices' forces are defeated.

Creon (who is Jocasta's brother and Antigone's uncle) becomes the new ruler of Thebes. His first order, or edict, forbids anyone to bury or mourn Polynices. This edict goes against established custom. Enemies who fall in battle are supposed to be honored by their relatives, given the customary rites, and buried. Antigone defies Creon's edict. She believes the gods demand that the burial customs be observed. She also wants to honor her fallen brother.

MATERIALS

Antigone (pages 48–54)
Making Masks (page 55)

HERE'S HOW

1 Read the introduction above to your class.

2 Assign roles for your students to play. Then have each actor construct a mask, according to directions from *Making Masks* on page 55. You may also want students to design a costume based on what they learned about Greek fashion on page 29.

3 Have students read or perform this adaptation of Sophocles' famous play *Antigone*. Lead them in a discussion about the play. Pose questions such as: In what ways are Antigone's values similar to ours today? How are they different? Was Creon wrong to expect obedience? Did he deserve his fate?

'NET LINKS

The Perseus Project provides a complete translation of Sophocles' *Antigone*:
http://www.perseus.tufts.edu/cgi-bin/text?lookup=soph.+ant.+1

Antigone

⌇ Adapted from the play by Sophocles ⌇

This famous Greek play is all about revenge, sacrifice, and death.

Cast of Characters:

Antigone (an-TIG-uh-nee), Creon's niece
Ismene (iz-MEE-nee), Antigone's sister
Chorus of Theban Elders
Creon (CREE-on), leader of Thebes
Watchman

Haemon (HEE-mon), Creon's son
Tiresias (ty-REE-sih-us), a blind seer
Messenger
Eurydice (yew-RID-uh-see),
    Creon's wife and Haemon's mother

All scenes are set in and around the wealthy dwelling of Creon of Thebes.

◈ SCENE I ◈

[*Enter Antigone and Ismene*]

Antigone: Ismene, my own sister by blood, Zeus has sent every evil possible to us, the children of Oedipus (ED-uh-pus).

Ismene: Is there some new trouble, sister?

Antigone: Yes. Creon, the leader of Thebes, has decreed that no one can bury our brother Polynices (pol-uh-NY-seez) because he led the attack against our city.

Ismene: But that decree flies in the face of Zeus himself. Everyone must be tended to and buried as a way of honoring the gods. Creon is our uncle. Surely he will change his mind.

Antigone: I doubt it. He has said that it would be death for anyone who disobeys. However, we must disobey, Sister, in order to fulfill our family obligations and to obey the gods.

Ismene: You can't be serious!

Antigone: I'm perfectly serious, but I can see by that look on your face that you won't help me. Very well. Even if you begged me now, I would not let you share in this honor.

[Exit Antigone and Ismene]

❖ SCENE II ❖

[Enter Chorus]

Chorus: Our poor city has suffered greatly in recent months. A terrible war between Oedipus' two sons, Eteocles (ee-TEE-oh-kleez) and Polynices, has destroyed much. The fighting began after the two brothers quarreled with each other. Polynices left, but he returned shortly with an army bent on destroying or enslaving our beloved Thebes. Eteocles and Polynices killed each other during the horrible battle that followed. The wise and noble Creon, their uncle, has been our leader since.

[Enter Creon]

Creon: Gentlemen of Thebes—I have decided to bury the body of noble Eteocles, who fought for his people, with full honors. But his brother Polynices shall remain unburied. His body shall be left outside the city to be consumed by dogs and birds. That disgrace is the least we can repay him for attacking this city and trying to destroy us.

Chorus: Your word is law to us all, Creon. We will obey.
[Enter Watchman]

Watchman: I tremble to tell you, master, that someone has already sprinkled dust on the body of Polynices to prepare it for burial.

Creon: What? Someone has helped that traitor to this city? Who would defy my order?

Watchman: I don't know. It happened quickly while the other watchmen and I were not looking.

Chorus: This might be the work of the gods.

Creon: Quiet, you silly old fools. It is not the gods but some more earthly source. Was it you, Watchman? Were you bribed by someone?

Watchman: Not I.

Creon: Then find me the people who did this, or you will suffer their fate.

[Exit Watchman]

◈ SCENE III ◈

[Enter Watchman with Antigone]

Watchman: This is the person who disobeyed your order, sir. We caught her while she was trying to finish the job of burying the body.

Creon: This woman is engaged to my son! Are you sure?

Antigone: He tells the truth, Uncle. I was burying Polynices.

Creon: Then, Watchman, you are free to go. Why did you do this, Antigone? Did you not understand my decree?

Antigone: I understood. But the gods have their own decrees, and I am bound to follow them. Also, he was my brother. Love and duty compelled me to give him a proper burial.

Creon: You foolish girl. You have killed yourself.

Antigone: Death will be welcome since I live among so many cowards. Had I left my brother's corpse alone, I would have had sorrow. But now I have none.

Chorus: She is a savage girl who is not bent by suffering.

[Enter Ismene]

Creon: And I suppose your sister Ismene helped you out?

Ismene: Yes, I did!

Antigone: No, she did not. I acted alone.

Creon: Your sister has proven that she is sympathetic to you. She will share your fate.

Ismene: Do what you want with me. I don't care. But why would you kill Antigone when she is engaged to your own son?

Creon: I would be disgraced to have my son married to such a disobedient, disrespectful woman. Guards, take them away.

[*Exit Antigone and Ismene*]

Chorus: The house of Oedipus is assailed by fate once more. When a family is shaken by the gods, there is no misfortune that is missed for generations to come.

◈ SCENE IV ◈

Haemon: No wedding to Antigone is worth as much as the noble example you give, Father.

Creon: I am glad to hear you say that, son. You would not want to marry such a girl. A bad relative is like a festering wound. And besides, we cannot appear to be giving in to the wishes of a mere woman.

Chorus: Your words are wise, sir.

Haemon: However, I have heard, Father, that the people of Thebes secretly support Antigone. They think she has behaved nobly and upheld her family duties. If you showed mercy, they would almost surely support you.

Chorus: These are also wise words, sir.

Creon: Am I to be taught by this mere boy?

Haemon: Judge me by my actions, not by my age, Father.

Creon: And am I to be led by the people or am I to lead them?

Haemon: You ignore their wishes at your own peril.

Creon: You support Antigone, too, don't you? It is she you are thinking of.

Haemon: I am thinking of you both.

Creon: Ismene may live. But Antigone must perish for what she has done. She will be walled up in a cave and left to die. Guards, carry out the order at once!

◈ SCENE V ◈

[*Enter Tiresias*]

Creon: Venerable Tiresias, what brings you here?

Tiresias: You have always listened to my prophecies in the past, and you have always heeded them, have you not?

Creon: Yes, of course.

Tiresias: And they have always benefited our city, do you agree?

Creon: Yes, why do you ask?

Tiresias: Because fate is about to cut you down.

Creon: What? I shiver at your words!

Tiresias: None of our sacrifices are being accepted by the gods. No bird in its screeching gives us favorable signs since they have been devouring the body of Polynices. Mark my words, Creon. Everyone makes mistakes. But after a mistake has been made, a person is no longer luckless or thoughtless if he tries to cure the ill he created.

Creon: Even you and your prophecies are against me! Did Antigone bribe you to say this? What tricks are you up to?

Tiresias: You are being a fool!

Creon: You cannot scare me or buy me!

Tiresias: Very well, I will pronounce your sentence. You will not live even another day before you see your own son dead. And there will be loud shrieks and moans from your own house as the Furies of Hades catch you and destroy your family.

[*Exit Tiresias*]

Chorus: This seer has never been wrong before, sir.

Creon: I know and my heart is troubled. What should I do?

Chorus: You should accept good counsel and undo your wrongs quickly.

Creon: Come, guards, let us go and free Antigone from the cave and go bury the body of Polynices.

[*Exit Creon and the guards*]

Chorus: May the gods wing them on their way.

◈ SCENE VI ◈

[*Enter Messenger*]

Chorus: Tell us, what news is there of Creon?

Messenger: Before today, I always believed Creon was a man to be envied. But now all is gone. I do not think he is a living man but a walking corpse.

Chorus: What grief do you carry for us?

Messenger: Death. And the dead accuse the living. Haemon is dead—killed by his own hand.

[*Enter Eurydice*]

Eurydice: What is this about my son?

Messenger: I attended your husband as we went to the place where the ghastly body of Polynices lay. We quickly performed the correct rituals and buried the body. Next, we went to the stone-lined cave where Antigone was buried alive. We opened up the cave to find her hanging by the neck from a noose made out of her own clothes.

Eurydice: And what of Haemon?

Messenger: The boy gave no answer but looked at Creon and spat in his face. Then he drew his sword and, before anyone could stop him, he plunged it into his side. Then he grabbed Antigone's body and died in that embrace.

[*Exit Eurydice*]

Chorus: The lady leaves without speaking. And here comes her husband now. Leave us, Messenger, lest your presence disturb him further.

[*Exit Messenger, following Eurydice; Enter Creon*]

Creon: I have killed my son, and I lament for all my errors. What a dreadful learning! It was a god who attacked me and stamped on my joy!

[*Re-enter Messenger*]

Messenger: Master, I come bearing even more bad news.

Creon: What disaster could possibly match this?

Messenger: Your wife has died from her own hand. Her last words were cursing you for taking away her son.

Creon: Now I am completely lost. I will not see another sunrise. My boy! I did not mean to hurt you. Now I have nothing to hold on to. Everything went wrong while it was in my hands. It was as if a heavy fate I could not carry leapt upon me.

[*Exit Creon*]

Chorus: Judgment is the greater part of good fortune. You cannot disrespect the gods, for the great words of a boastful person will be repaid with great blows. And this, as one grows old, teaches judgement.

THE END

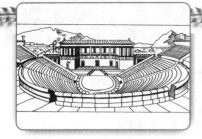

Making Masks

Greek drama relied on few props, but all characters wore costumes. In ancient Greece, actors covered their head and face with masks that were often quite elaborate. For this production, your students can create and use handheld masks.

MATERIALS

sturdy white paper
tape
scissors
colored markers
rulers or sticks about one foot long
[For each character in the play you will need one wooden ruler or stick and one piece of sturdy white paper. In addition to the Chorus, there are eight characters. The Chorus can be as large or as small as needed.]

HERE'S HOW

1 Conduct a read-through of the play. Those students who do not volunteer for or have not been assigned roles can be involved in the chorus. You also may want students to share a role so that more students have a chance to participate in lead speaking parts.

2 On the white paper, have students (including chorus members) draw an oval large enough to cover their faces. They may use markers to design a mask that they believe sums up their character. Be sure to have students cut out eyeholes so that they can see where they're going.

3 After students have cut out the faces that they drew, instruct them to tape a ruler or stick to the back of their masks. A few inches should stick out from the bottom of the mask for use as a handle.

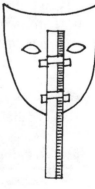

4 Throughout the play, the actors should use the ruler or stick as a handle to hold the mask over their faces. Make sure they speak loudly since the masks will undoubtedly muffle their voices.

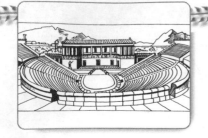

The Seven Wonders of the Ancient World

The Seven Wonders of the Ancient World is a group of truly impressive structures built between about 2600 and 200 B.C. Since the list was created by the ancient Greeks, it is not surprising that it included mostly Greek structures. Five of the seven wonders owe their existence to the Greeks' genius for architecture and building.

MATERIALS

The Seven Wonders of the Ancient World (pages 57 and 58)

HERE'S HOW

1 Pass out copies of The Seven Wonders of the Ancient World. Have students use the map and an encyclopedia or other resources to unscramble the names of the seven wonders. Then they can match each name to its description. You might pose the follow-up questions (see #3 below) at the end of the exercise.

2 Develop a class list of "The Seven Wonders of the Modern World." Students can research and report briefly on one "wonder" they have selected and present reasons why it should be included on the list. Then a class vote can be taken. Alternatively, each student or pair of students might develop an illustrated threefold pamphlet that describes in tour-guide fashion the seven modern wonders they have chosen.

3 Pose the following questions to generate discussion about the Seven Wonders of the Ancient World:

※ Which five wonders were built or designed by Greeks? (Numbers 3–7, pages 57 and 58)

※ Why do you think ancient people decided that these creations were the seven greatest wonders of their time? (Answers may vary. The ancient Greeks might have selected these structures because they were impressive, complicated, and expensive projects that were unique in some way.)

'NET LINKS

This excellent Web site gives a brief history of the Seven Wonders of the Ancient World as well as some fanciful drawings of what they might have looked like: **http://ce.eng.usf.edu/pharos/wonders/**

ANSWER KEY: The Seven Wonders of the Ancient World (pages 57 and 58)

Word Scramble

A. Temple of Artemis at Ephesus
B. Colossus of Rhodes
C. Hanging Gardens of Babylon
D. Lighthouse of Alexandria
E. Statue of Zeus at Olympia
F. Pyramids at Giza
G. Mausoleum at Halicarnassus

Matching

1. F; 2. C; 3. A; 4. E; 5. G; 6. B; 7. D

The Seven Wonders of the Ancient World
⌐ Ancient Momuments ⌐

Use the map below and an encyclopedia or other resource to help you unscramble the names of the Seven Wonders of the Ancient World. Then match the name with the descriptive paragraph below.

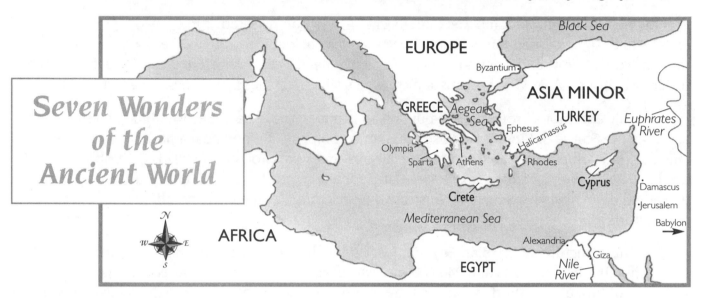

Word Scramble Use the map to help you figure out the last word in each phrase: the location of the Wonder.

A. pleemt fo mirtsae ta hesepus _____

B. sucosols fo dehors _____

C. gihngan nsrdgae fo olbyabn _____

D. thligseouh fo iadxlerana _____

E. tuesta fo usze ta iyampol _____

F. mipadyrs ta izga _____

G. leuumasmo ta asharnsusical _____

Matching Write the letter for each Wonder from the Word Scramble next to the matching description below.

_____ **1.** Built in Egypt around 2600 B.C., these are the oldest of the seven wonders. They were designed to be tombs for kings, but they became a popular tourist site for Greeks and Romans thousands of years later. This is the only Wonder that can still be seen today.

_____ **2.** These were probably built between 605 and 562 B.C. by King Nebuchadnezzar II for one of his many wives. Reportedly, he married a mountain princess and wanted her to feel at home. However, very little is known about this "green" Wonder, including when or how it was destroyed.

_____ **3.** Built around 550 B.C. by Croesus, king of Lydia, this was one of the biggest and most complicated temples ever made. It was constructed in a Greek city in what is today western Turkey. In 356 B.C., the temple burned down, but it was quickly rebuilt. It was burned down several other times before finally being destroyed by invading Goths in A.D. 262.

The Seven Wonders of the Ancient World (cont.)

_____ **4.** This was the most famous statue in the ancient world. Created by a Greek sculptor around 435 B.C., the 40-foot statue showed the chief Greek god sitting on a huge throne. His clothes were made of gold and his flesh of ivory. Eventually, a massive fire destroyed the statue in A.D. 462.

_____ **5.** This giant marble tomb was built in what is now southwestern Turkey. Two famous Greek architects designed it and four famous Greek sculptors helped decorate it. The structure was so impressive that now all decorated tombs carry its name. It was damaged in an earthquake and then torn down around A.D. 1500 by Christian crusaders who used the marble to build a fortress.

_____ **6.** This enormous bronze statue built on an island in the Aegean Sea was 120 feet tall—about as big as the Statue of Liberty. And like the Statue of Liberty, it stood near a harbor and greeted ships as they came and went. Created by a famous Greek sculptor around 282 B.C., it only survived until 224 B.C., when an earthquake toppled it. People planned to rebuild the statue, but a soothsayer warned them against trying to reconstruct the structure. The metal eventually was sold for scrap a few centuries later.

_____ **7.** This structure stood in an Egyptian harbor and had a practical function—to guide ships. It was completed between 283 and 246 B.C. and was designed by a Greek architect. It was more than 400 feet tall (about one-third as high as the Empire State Building), making it the tallest structure in the ancient world. It stood for several centuries but was badly damaged by earthquakes and poor management. Around A.D. 1480, the Muslim ruler of Egypt tore it down completely and rebuilt it as a fort.

Name the Wonder!

_____   _____   _____   _____

_____   _____   _____   _____

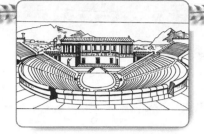

Pythagoras I: Creating a Builder's Triangle
~ *Ancient Greek Engineering* ~

The following two exercises focus on the Greek mathematician Pythagoras and the Pythagorean theorem. Pythagoras' famous theorem was based on a kind of right triangle well known to ancient builders and craftspeople. It was used constantly to build houses, temples, and structures of all kinds. The "Builder's Triangle" had a special set of measurements: Its sides had 3, 4, and 5 equally spaced units, as shown on the next page. Ancient builders could easily create such a triangle using a knotted loop of rope and some stakes. The rope had 12 evenly spaced knots and the stakes were adjusted to create the 3-4-5 measurements. Using it, builders made sure that corners and joints were at perfect 90-degree angles. Create your own Builder's Triangle for the class using these materials.

MATERIALS

pushpins and bulletin-board space (or geoboards)
spool of white string
felt-tip pens or markers
rulers
unlined paper
tape (optional)

HERE'S HOW

1 Provide each student with a piece of string that measures about 1½ feet, a ruler, a pen or marker, paper, and tape. Students will also need access to a bulletin board with pushpins or to a geoboard.

2 Model the directions that follow (numbers 3–5) for your students. You can make your demonstration easy to see by changing the measurements below from inches to feet to create a giant triangle with a 12-foot perimeter. Alternatively, you can use string, a transparent ruler, and water-based markers on a transparency for the overhead projector.

3 Line up your length of string with the inch marks on the ruler, making sure plenty of excess string extends from both ends of the ruler. Take the pen and mark the string at the 0 mark and every inch mark from 1 to 12. There should be 13 marks on your string altogether. Tie both ends of the string together so that the first and last marks are joined in a knot. You should now have a loop with 12 marks that are equidistant from one another.

4 Stick one of the pins into the bulletin board (you may also use tape to fasten the string). Take the loop and hook it around the pin at one of the marks—the top of your triangle. Stick in the next pin 4 marks below and hook the string around this pin. Follow the string 3 marks to the left or right and place your last pin to form a base that is 3 marks long and a hypotenuse (the diagonal) that is 5 marks long. Wrap the string around the three pins to form a triangle. Adjust the pins if necessary to create a 3-4-5 pattern of marks.

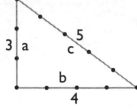

5. You now have a Builder's Triangle. The angle that is opposite the hypotenuse, the line with five marks, is a right angle.

6. You can also demonstrate with the Builder's Triangle how to make a right angle from any straight line: Use your ruler to draw a long horizontal line on a piece of paper. Tape the piece of paper onto your bulletin board. Place one pin at the far left point of the line. Loop your Builder's Triangle over that pin and then follow the string straight across the line 4 marks. Place a pin at the fourth mark and loop the string around it. Finally, bring the remaining length of the loop straight down 3 marks and place a pin at this third mark. The loop should be fully stretched out. You should now have a right angle at the vertex where the 4-inch and the 3-inch sides meet. The side with five units should run opposite this angle.

7. Encourage students to use their Builder's Triangles to draw right angles for other lines and experiment with this tool. Using a geoboard is the easiest way to experiment accurately without using pins.

Who Was Pythagoras?

Pythagoras (pih-THAG-uhr-us) was born on the island of Samos about 570 B.C. He is one of the most influential—and most mysterious—figures in Greek history. Not only was he a great mathematician and philosopher, he was also the founder of a small movement that was half-religious and half-scientific. In later years the group became famous for its offbeat rules and beliefs. Pythagoreans were secretive folk who refused to eat meat because they believed human souls were reincarnated as animals. They also believed that all numbers had their own personality—beautiful or ugly, masculine or feminine—and that all relationships could be reduced to numbers. Pythagoras' famous theorem was actually known to the Babylonians and Egyptians at least 1,000 years before his time. However, Pythagoras is believed to have been the first person to prove it was true. Because of the many myths and legends surrounding Pythagoras, experts are not sure when he died. But his movement—which included both men and women—lived on for several hundred years.

LIBRARY LINKS

A nicely illustrated book called *Technology in the Time of Ancient Greece* by Judith Crosher gives an overview of the know-how behind everything from Greek pottery to shipbuilding. More advanced students should look for *The Ancient Engineers* by L. Sprague de Camp.

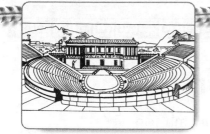

Pythagoras II: The Theorem
⌒ Ancient Greek Math ⌒

Many of your students may already be familiar with the Pythagorean theorem. Adjust your lesson plan to reflect their level of understanding.

MATERIALS

The Pythagorean Theorem (pages 62 and 63)
calculator with a square root function

HERE'S HOW

1 Review the Ideas to Know section below with your students. If students have worked with the Builder's Triangle (pages 59 and 60), they will have a better understanding of the principles behind the theorem.

2 Pass out copies of The Pythagorean Theorem. Depending on the needs of your students, either talk them through or have them work independently on the first portion of their activity sheet. This should help solidify their understanding of the Pythagorean theorem.

3 Set aside time for students to answer independently all the questions that follow. They will need a calculator to complete number 10 and the bonus question.

IDEAS TO KNOW

✳ *Right triangle*: Any triangle containing one 90° angle. The sides of the triangle are usually labeled a, b, and c. (See example on page 62.)

✳ *Hypotenuse*: The side of a right triangle that is opposite the 90° angle. It is usually side c.

✳ *Square*: The amount of any number multiplied by itself. For example, the square of 4 is 16 because 4 X 4 = 16. The square of 4 is expressed as 4^2.

✳ *Square root*: The reverse of a square. The square root of 16 is 4 because 4 X 4 = 16. The square root of 16 is expressed as $\sqrt{16}$.

✳ *The Pythagorean theorem*: For any right triangle, the length of the hypotenuse squared (c^2) will equal the squares of the other two sides added together ($a^2 + b^2$). Putting it all together, the theorem is expressed as $c^2 = a^2 + b^2$.

ANSWER KEY The Pythagorean Theorem (page 63)
1. 9; 2. 16; 3. 25; 4. 3; 5. 4; 6. 5; 7. 25; 8. 5; 9. 74; 10. 8.60

Bonus question
Use the commutative property, as shown below, to solve this problem:
$4^2 - 3^2 = a^2$
$16 - 9 = a^2$
$5 = a^2$
$\sqrt{5} = a$
$2.23 = a$

Name _____   Date _____

The Pythagorean Theorem

To understand how the Pythagorean theorem works, read this information.

This is a drawing of a right triangle.
Notice that its sides (a, b, and c) are in
the shape of a Builder's Triangle.
They are 3, 4, and 5 units long.

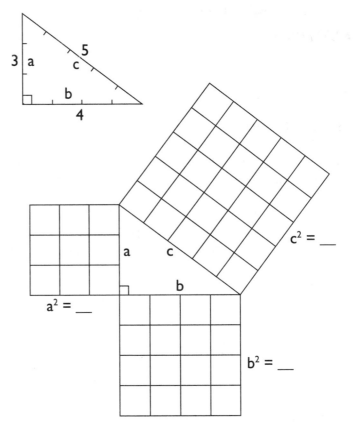

Using the measurements from this
triangle, the Pythagorean theorem
($c^2 = a^2 + b^2$) would read $5^2 = 3^2 + 4^2$.
With its sides squared, the triangle
would now look like this:

Now follow these steps:

1. Count up the number of little boxes in the side **a** square, and write that number on the blank to show **a²**.

2. Take your answer for **a²**, and write the letter "a" that many times in the empty boxes in the side **c** square.

3. Repeat the steps above (numbers 1 and 2), using the side **b** square to find **b²**. Be sure to fill the correct number of unmarked boxes in the side **c** square with the letter "b."

What did you find?

_____

_____

cal language: $c^2 = a^2 + b^2$.

problem. The two smaller squares can be cut up and used to fill up the larger square exactly. Today we express the same thought using mathemati-

The 25 boxes in the side **c** square should be filled with either an "a" or "b" (9 **a** boxes plus 16 **b** boxes). This is how Pythagoras would have seen the

The Pythagorean Theorem (cont.)

Now use what you have learned about the Pythagorean theorem to answer the following questions. You may need a calculator to complete number 10 and the bonus question.

1. What is 3^2?

_____

2. What is 4^2?

_____

3. What is 5^2?

_____

Pythagoras

4. What is the square root of 9?

_____

Work Space

5. What is the square root of 16?

_____

6. What is the square root of 25?

_____

7. If $c^2 = 3^2 + 4^2$, how much is c^2?

_____

8. If $c^2 = 3^2 + 4^2$, how much is c?

_____

9. If $c^2 = 5^2 + 7^2$, how much is c^2?

_____

10. If $c^2 = 5^2 + 7^2$, how much is c?

_____

Bonus question

In the previous questions, you were solving to find the length of the hypotenuse, or "c." How would you solve to find "a" in the following equation: $4^2 = a^2 + 3^2$?

Answer:

CHAPTER 5

A Closer Look: Athens Versus Sparta

Democracy, Social Order, and Justice

Athens and Sparta were the two most famous city-states in ancient Greece, and they were separated by more than just rugged mountains and coastline. Boasting completely different societies, they carried on one of the greatest rivalries in history.

Athens was a prosperous, outgoing democracy that spread its influence and its policies as far as possible. The Athenians' direct democracy, in which even the humblest citizen could vote on important issues, was considered rowdy by many other Greeks. Yet it helped make Athens prosperous and powerful. Of course, not everyone enjoyed freedom in Athens. Women were largely expected to stay at home, and they had few rights. Some slaves lived comfortable lives, but many lived much worse than any slaves in the Deep South before the Civil War. Nevertheless, Athens was far ahead of its time in its system of justice and patronage of the arts. When we think of our rich Greek heritage, we think of Athens.

The Spartans were, first and last, warriors. Their entire society was geared toward raising and training soldiers, and their government was a tightly controlled oligarchy. All this made the Spartans conservative and inward-looking. Spartan infants had to be examined by city elders shortly after birth. If they were found to be physically defective, they were left on a mountainside to die. At the age of seven, Spartan boys were taken from their mothers and put through rigorous physical training. They had to exercise constantly and sleep outside in all types of weather. They were given only one cloak to wear and they were deliberately underfed. Boys were expected to make up for their lack of food by stealing. If they were caught, they were severely beaten. This hard conditioning, as well as constant military drills, made Spartans the most feared land warriors in Greece from about 600 B.C. to 371 B.C.

Ironically, Sparta—one of Greece's most repressive city-states—allowed the greatest freedom for its women. Women could own land, and they were expected to get out and exercise so that they could bear healthy children. This small degree of freedom scandalized men from other Greek city-states. If it's possible, though, the Spartans treated their slaves even more harshly than the Athenians did. Called "Helots," Spartan slaves were owned by the state and controlled by terror. Young Spartan boys were encouraged to stalk and kill helots—especially troublemakers—to hone their warrior skills.

During the Persian War that lasted roughly from 500 to 479 B.C., Athens and Sparta cooperated with each other to help drive away the hated Persians. Once that threat was over though, the tensions between them rose until it exploded into the Peloponnesian War in 431 B.C. After decades of fighting, Athens finally lost the war in 404 B.C. Sparta stripped the Athenians of their power, but allowed the city to survive. In time, Athens revived itself though it never achieved its former glory. However, Sparta suffered a worse fate; when Sparta lost to Thebes in 371 B.C., the power and influence of this city-state were shattered for good.

Who's the Winner?

~ *Cultural, Political, and Social Contrast:* ~
Athens and Sparta

A Venn diagram is a useful tool for helping students find out how daily life differed in Greece's two greatest city-states, Athens and Sparta.

MATERIALS

Who's the Winner? (pages 67 and 68)

HERE'S HOW

1 Distribute a copy of *Who's the Winner?* to each student.

2 Instruct the class to compare the two lists containing information about Athens and Sparta. Then challenge students to put the categories in the appropriate place on the Venn diagram. Remind students that they should not put a category in the "both" column unless the two sides match exactly.

3 Have students use the finished diagram and the map to answer the questions on the activity sheet.

'NET LINKS

There are several good Web sites that can help students get acquainted with ancient Athens and Sparta. Here are four of the best:

http://www.wsu.edu:8080/~dee/GREECE/GREECE.HTM
(Presents the best overall introduction to Athens and Sparta)

http://www.indiana.edu/~kglowack/athens/ (Provides a virtual tour of Athens as it was)

http://www.ancientsites.com/xi/places/home/index.rage?loc=Athens
(Presents daily life in Athens, including walking tours)

http://homer.reed.edu/Parthenon.html (Focuses on the Parthenon)

ANSWER KEY *Who's the Winner?* (page 68)

1. Language, chief god, most important literary works
2. Athens—it had more trade with other places, while Sparta discouraged trade.
3. Athens—they lived in a democracy.
4. Sparta—they were given freedom to do a wider range of activities.
5. Athenian boys—they were the only ones allowed to go to school.
6. Spartan boys—most of their activities were military in nature.
7. Because Sparta had Greece's most powerful army
8. Sparta—slaves outnumbered citizens by a much larger number, and young boys had to help keep slaves in line.
9. Athens—it's main religious site was dedicated to the goddess of wisdom.
10. Athens—it used silver coins instead of heavy lead bars.
11. Athens—it had a powerful navy and relied heavily on trade.

Name _____   Date _____

Who's the Winner?

Fill in the Venn diagram below using this information.

	ATHENS	SPARTA
Language:	Greek	Greek
Estimated free population (adult males only):	45,000	25,000
Estimated population of slaves:	75,000	250,000
Form of government:	democracy	oligarchy
Main form of money:	silver coins called *drachmas*	heavy iron bars called *obols*
Chief god:	Zeus	Zeus
Important religious site:	the Parthenon—dedicated to Athena, the goddess of wisdom	shrines to the minor gods Fear, Laughter, and Death
Major exports:	silver, olives, olive oil, wine, pottery	the Spartans discouraged all trade with foreigners
Major imports:	slaves, timber, corn, iron, tin	
Best-known literary works:	Homer's *Iliad* and *Odyssey*	Homer's *Iliad* and *Odyssey*
Age when men become full citizens:	18	30
Typical childhood activities (boys):	going to school, exercising, learning military drills, playing with friends	exercising, learning military drills, stealing food to survive, hunting and killing rebellious slaves, policing slaves to keep them in line
Typical childhood activities (girls):	learning household duties	exercising, athletic competitions, learning household duties
Military strong point:	Greece's most powerful navy	Greece's most powerful army

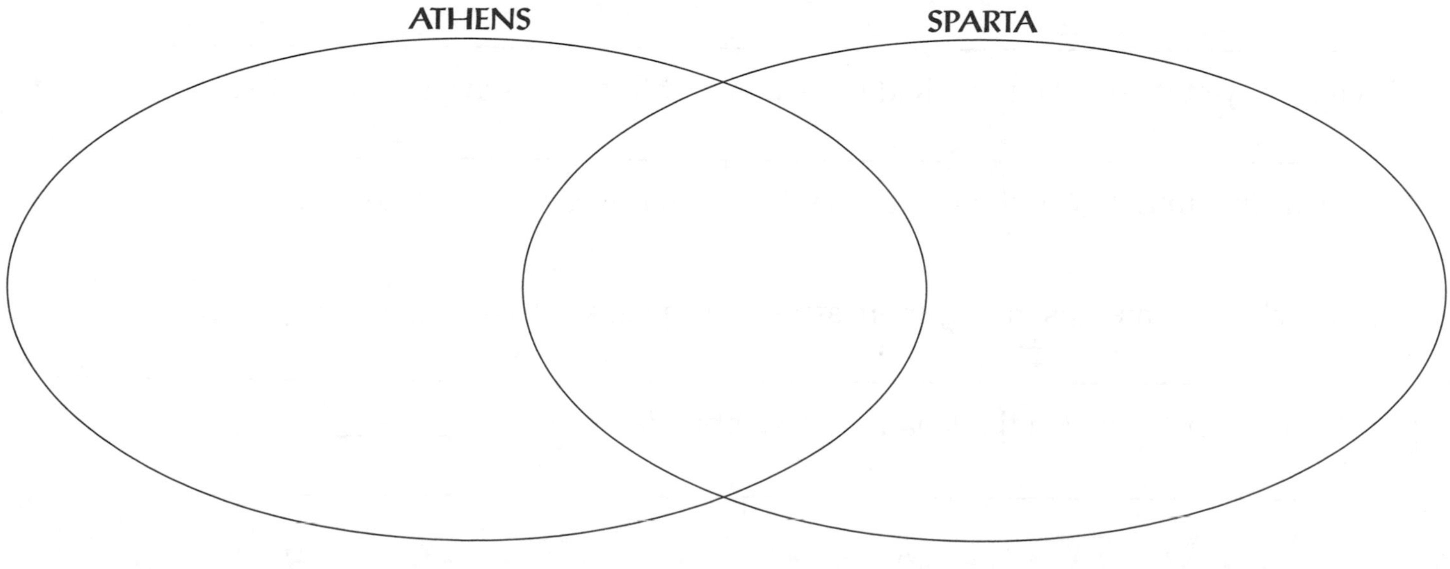

ATHENS   SPARTA

Who's the Winner? (cont.)

Use the information in your diagram and on the map to help you answer these questions.

1 What important things did Athens and Sparta share?

_____

_____

_____

_____

2 Did Athens or Sparta have more contact with foreigners? Explain. _____

_____

3 In which city-state did adult males probably have more freedom? Explain. _____

_____

4 In which city-state did young girls have more freedom? Explain. _____

_____

5 Which group of young people in the two city-states was the best educated? Explain. _____

_____

_____

6 Which group of young people in the two city-states received more training to fight and kill? Explain. _____

_____

7 Why was such training important to that city-state? _____

_____

8 Which city-state do you think had more of a problem with slave revolts? Explain. _____

_____

9 Which city-state do you think put a greater emphasis on wisdom? Explain. _____

_____

10 In which city-state was money more attractive and easier to use? Explain. _____

_____

11 Which city-state do you think had more shipbuilders? Explain. _____

_____

Go Tell the Spartans

⤳ *Ancient Spartan Military Strategy* ⤳

Sparta was a military state that was famous for its secrecy. So it makes sense that one of the few surviving bits of information about Sparta is a military code. The key to using the Spartan code was a *scytale*, or wooden staff. If the Spartans wanted to send a message, they wrapped a long, narrow piece of parchment around the scytale and wrote the message in vertical columns. (See the drawing below.) When unraveled, the strip of parchment looked like a string of unrelated letters. But when the parchment was sent to another Spartan commander, it was wrapped around a scytale of identical width and was easily read.

MATERIALS
♦ ♦ ♦ ♦ ♦ ♦ ♦ ♦ ♦ ♦ ♦

two (or more) scytales*
scissors
ruler
11x17 sheets of paper cut into long strips (about ½ inch wide)

HERE'S HOW
♦ ♦ ♦ ♦ ♦ ♦ ♦ ♦ ♦ ♦ ♦ ♦

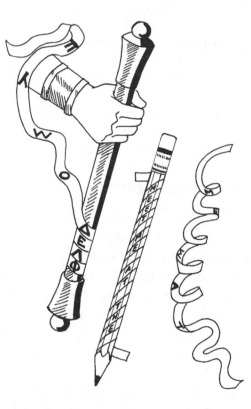

1 Show the students the scytale model you'll use. Explain briefly what it is and how to write a message on it.

2 Either pass out prepared slips of paper or have students cut out their own. Pass around the scytales and have students use them to write their names and full addresses or brief messages. Remind them to write their messages vertically, in rows.

3 While the scytales are making the rounds, provide students with some background information about Sparta (see next page and chapter introduction, page 64) and why such a code would have been important to the Spartans.

4 When students have finished writing their messages, have them hand their strips of paper to the front of the room. Mix the papers up and pass them out to the class at random. Then hand the *scytales* around again and let students read their strips of paper. While that is going on, continue with your discussion of Sparta.

*Note: You will need at least two or three scytales. They should be cylindrical and about six to eight inches long, and can be any width (note that it is easier to write on a thicker cylinder). However, it is vital that they all be of identical lengths and widths so that students can exchange messages. You can cut up an old broom handle or go to a local hardware store or lumberyard and have dowels cut. For a less-expensive alternative, ask for donations of empty paper-towel rolls. In a pinch, even pencils can serve as scytales (students will simply have to write smaller). You will also need long, narrow strips of paper, as described in the materials list.

SPARTAN SECRECY

The Spartans were a famously conservative and tight-lipped bunch. Foreigners were closely watched and thrown out of town from time to time, apparently to keep them from learning too much. The historian Thucydides expressed repeated frustration with them as he wrote his history of the war between Sparta and Athens. "The secrecy with which their affairs are conducted meant that no one knew the numbers of the Spartans," he explained.

The Spartans had a good reason to be secretive: They did not have very many citizen soldiers, or "equals." In part that is because Sparta's land-inheritance rules discouraged large families. At the beginning of the war between Sparta and Athens, Athens outnumbered Sparta by about 13,000 soldiers to 4,000. The philosopher Aristotle said that by the time Sparta's power fell apart in 371 B.C., the Spartans had a hard time fielding just 1,000 equals, though Sparta still controlled enough land to support 30,000.

WHO WERE THE SPARTANS?

Military drilling and harsh conditioning earned the Spartans a fierce reputation around the Mediterranean. If Spartans did not win a battle, they were expected to fight to the last man rather than surrender. That did not always happen, but often it did. The most famous instance came in 480 B.C. at Thermopylae against the Persians. There, a special monument was erected that read: "Go tell the Spartans, you who read/We took their orders and are dead."

LACONIC COMMENTS

Aside from their awesome army, Spartans were famous for coining snappy one-liners. Since Sparta is located in a region called Laconia, these one-liners became known among ancient Greeks (and to us) as laconic comments. Some of them were amusing. One Spartan saw his son fighting recklessly and told him, "Either increase your strength or reduce your self-confidence." Another time, a Spartan king was asked if he was keeping quiet because he was stupid or because he was at a loss for words. He replied: "A stupid person wouldn't be able to keep quiet."

Most laconic comments were intended to be profound, and one of the best known came from a wife and mother. As her son marched off to war, she supposedly said: "Son, either with this or on this." The "this" she referred to was his shield, which was the first thing that defeated soldiers threw away. (It was hard for a fleeing soldier carrying a shield to gain speed and escape death or capture from the victors.) The mother in this story was telling her son to come back carrying the shield in victory or to come back dead, laid out on his shield.*

---

* Historians say that there are some problems with this quote's authenticity. First, Spartans were usually buried where they died, not returned home. Second, the round shields used by Greek soldiers were not very useful as stretchers for carrying the wounded or dead. Even so, the quote summarizes the attitude a good Spartan was supposed to have about war: victory or death.

Murder in Athens!
Part I: Athenian Justice
∽ Athenian Justice Compared With U.S. Justice ∽

The activity *Murder in Athens!* comes in three sections. The first is designed to acquaint students with the Athenian justice system. The second allows them to re-create the events that led to an actual trial. And the third is a re-creation of the trial itself, which took place some time between 450 and 411 B.C.

MATERIALS

Murder in Athens! Part I: Athenian Justice Versus U.S. Justice (page 73)

HERE'S HOW

1 Introduce your students to the information on Athenian democracy contained in the information below and in the introduction to this chapter (page 64). Be sure to point out that Athens invented democracy, which for the first time allowed ordinary people to make laws and see them carried out in the courts.

2 Distribute *Murder in Athens! Part I: Athenian Justice Versus U.S. Justice* and encourage students to read and comment on the chart, which compares ancient Athenian and modern U.S. criminal justice systems.

3 Help students grasp the differences and similarities between the Athenian system of justice and the one we use today. Pose the following questions to students to initiate a discussion or write the questions on the board, discuss them, and have students write responses. Either way, their ability to compare and contrast the two justice systems will be vital for *Murder in Athens! Part III: The Trial of Daphne.*

Questions:

※ Name at least three similarities you find between the ancient Athenian and modern U.S. justice systems.

※ What are the major differences? List three to five differences. Choose what you believe is the most important difference and explain why this difference is important.

※ Which system do you think is better? Explain and give examples.

LAND WITHOUT LAWYERS

There were no lawyers in ancient Greece. However, ordinary citizens facing a trial had several ways to prepare for their day in court. The art of public speaking, or rhetoric, was a big part of every young man's basic education, like math is today. That was vital because most trials hinged on the speeches given by the prosecutor or the defense. Even so, most people needed help in finding the right words to say, so both sides hired professional writers to compose their speeches to the jury.

THE GREAT OUTDOORS

Imagine seeing a crime show on TV where the trials are held outside. That was standard procedure for murder trials in Athens, which were held in an outdoor court called the *Areopagus*. Why? In part because the Greeks believed that any person or object responsible for shedding blood had been polluted. That pollution was considered to be as dangerous as a disease. No member of the court wanted to be under the same roof as a murderer.

SOLON, THANKS FOR THE MEMORIES

In 594 B.C., a prominent Athenian named Solon was given one year to reform Athens' legal code. The city was laboring under the harsh laws that punished almost all lawbreaking with the death penalty. Solon lightened many punishments and increased citizen representation in the law courts. After he finished that work, Solon left Athens for ten years because he was besieged by people either complaining about his new laws or wanting him to make changes. Despite those complaints, the jury system that Solon created remained largely in place for the next three centuries.

Murder in Athens! Part I:
∽ Athenian Justice Versus U.S. Justice ∽

Use this chart to compare the criminal justice system of ancient Athens with that of the United States today.

	ATHENS	UNITED STATES
Who decides the guilt or innocence of somebody accused of a crime?	A jury	A jury or, in some cases, a judge
How big are the juries?	100 to 2,000 people	Usually 12 people
Who can serve on a jury?	Adult male citizens (women, slaves, and children are excluded)	All adult citizens
How are verdicts reached?	By a majority vote (a tie vote means the accused person goes free)	By a unanimous vote (if the vote is not unanimous, the accused person is usually retried with a different jury)
Who prosecutes accused criminals in court?	If the victim of the crime is an adult male, then the victim himself prosecutes. If the victim is a woman or child—or if someone has been murdered—then the closest male relative prosecutes.	A publicly paid lawyer called a district attorney prosecutes.
Who handles the defense?	The person accused of the crime defends himself if he is an adult male. If the accused is a woman or child, then the closest male relative handles the defense.	Accused individuals usually hire a lawyer to defend them, although they are allowed to defend themselves.
Who makes sure the trial is fair?	A city official called a magistrate makes sure that the trial is orderly. But he cannot force the prosecutor or defense to follow laws governing trials.	A judge with legal training makes sure the law is followed and that both sides present a fair case.
How long do trials last?	Usually less than one day	Length varies; most usually last no longer than a week or two
What are their trials like?	Most trials revolve around two speeches, the first given by the prosecutor and the second by the defense. Both sides are allowed to call witnesses. However, the opposition is not allowed to question those witnesses.	The prosecution first tries to prove that the accused person is guilty by calling witnesses and presenting evidence. The defense then gets a chance to reply by calling its own witnesses and presenting its own evidence. Both sides are allowed to question the opposition's witnesses. And both sides can make speeches at the beginning and end of the trial.

Murder in Athens!
Part II: The Scene of the Crime
Part III: The Trial of Daphne
⁓ *Athenian Criminal Trial Simulation* ⁓

The goals of these two exercises are to teach students about Athens' justice system as well as to develop their writing and speaking skills. While this simulation is based on a real case (see Background, below), remind students that an actual murder trial in Athens would have been slightly more complex (involving preliminary hearings and witness testimony, for example). However, the case outlined below is very similar in structure to other Athenian trials.

Background

Sometime between 450 and 411 B.C., an Athenian jury meeting at the *Areopagus* (air-ee-OP-uh-gus) heard a murder trial about a woman accused of poisoning her husband and one of his friends. Antiphon, one of Athens' greatest legal speechwriters, wrote the address delivered by the prosecutor in that case. Antiphon's speech has been preserved, and it forms the basis for this mock trial. Unfortunately, no other information about his case—including the jury's verdict—has survived. Daphne (daf-NEE) is a made-up name for a real person, as are all but one of the names used in this mock trial.

MATERIALS
• • • • • • • • • • •

The materials for this trial can be as elaborate or as simple as you like. You can try to make the re-creation as authentic as possible, using costumes patterned after the designs on page 29, a water clock, and solid and hollow ballots for the jury (see projects described on page 80). Or you can have students act out the murder scene and the trial with few or no props at all. No matter how you do it, you will need the following:

Murder in Athens! Parts I, II, and III (pages 73 and 76–79)
a timepiece with a second hand
objects that jury members can use as ballots

HERE'S HOW
• • • • • • • • • • •

1 Distribute copies of *Murder in Athens!* Parts II and III to your students (they should already have a copy of *Part* I). After the class has read both parts, spend some time discussing the case. Then explain to students that they are going to put on a skit and mock trial based on this information.

2 Select a cast for your skit and mock trial. Work with students to decide how each part should be produced. You might want to have students create a list of the costumes and props they will need for both the skit and the trial. Then assign students to come up with each item.

3 Allow the students who are performing the skit some extra time to rehearse. The easiest way to handle the skit is to have a narrator read the text of *The Scene of the Crime* while the players silently act out the events. However, encourage students to be creative. The skit is designed to show other students what events led up to the crime, so tell the actors to highlight details. For instance, the couples could be bickering on their way to the feast to show that both relationships were rocky.

4 For the mock trial, the main responsibilities will fall on the two actors playing Milo and Leon (remember: these roles can be played by either boys or girls). They can either write their own speeches or—to be more authentic—have other students compose them. Greeks appearing in court would have memorized their speeches, but that is not necessary for this mock trial.

5 Both speeches should be no more than about five minutes long. Each one should briefly summarize the events that led up to the murder (the real jury would not have seen a skit) and explain why their side is right and the other side is wrong. The writers should have some leeway in interpreting the facts. But generally, they should stick to the facts of the case in their speeches. For the sake of accuracy, you may want to review the speeches before they are delivered.

6 The agenda for The Trial of Daphne is as follows:
  I. Prosecution speech
  II. Defense speech
  III. Jury vote
  IV. Verdict announced by magistrate

7 After the trial, ask jury members why they voted the way they did. Take a show of hands from all the students to see how they would have voted. Have them explain the reasons for their decision. Also, discuss what students think about the Athenian justice system. Is this a fair way to run a murder trial? Are there any advantages to the way it would have been handled in a modern U.S. criminal court?

THE DEATH PENALTY
◆ ◆ ◆ ◆ ◆ ◆ ◆ ◆ ◆ ◆ ◆ ◆ ◆ ◆ ◆ ◆ ◆ ◆

Athenian citizens found guilty of intentional murder faced the death penalty. It was administered in either of two forms: the first was drinking poisonous hemlock and the second was a type of strangulation or crucifixion.

LIBRARY LINKS
To read excerpts from Antiphon's actual speech, check out No. 76 in the book *Women's Life in Greece and Rome: A Source Book in Translation* by Mary R. Lefkowitz and Maureen B. Fant. For more general information on Athens during the Golden Age, look for *What Was Life Like at the Dawn of Democracy?* by the editors of Time-Life Books.

Murder in Athens! Part II:
∽ *The Scene of the Crime* ∽

In many plays it is the job of the narrator to set the scene for the events that follow. Read what the narrator below has to say.

Cast of Characters:

Timotheos (tim-AH-thay-ows) and **Philoneos** (fil-OH-ne-ows), two citizens of Athens who die under suspicious circumstances

Daphne (daf-NEE), Timotheos' wife

Themis (THEM-is), a slave and Philoneos' girlfriend

Four Guards, two carry off Themis to her execution and two arrest Daphne

(Note: All the names in the case, except that of Philoneos, have been lost to history. The rest are made-up names of real people.)

How It Happened:

Narrator: The two victims, Timotheos and Philoneos, were friends who both planned to make trips to far away cities. They decided to have a good-bye feast together with Daphne, Timotheos' wife, and Themis, Philoneos' slave and girlfriend. Timotheos and Daphne had been having marital trouble, and Philoneous and Themis had not been getting along well either. So before the feast, both women agreed that they needed to do something to save their relationships. They decided to give the men a love potion, a special powder that, if consumed, was believed to make someone fall head-over-heels in love. After Daphne obtained the potion in Athens, Themis slipped it into the men's drinks at dinner. Unfortunately, the potion turned out to be poisonous. Themis gave a bigger dose to Philoneos, her boyfriend, and he dropped dead immediately. Timotheos, who had a smaller dose, became ill and finally died after three weeks of intense suffering. Since Themis was a slave, she had no rights and was quickly executed for her part in killing two men. Daphne insisted that she thought the poison was truly a love potion. Since she was the wife of a citizen, she had to be put on trial. . . . Your class will play the part of the jury. If you find her guilty, she will be executed.

Murder in Athens! Part III:
⇜ The Trial of Daphne ⇝

This murder trial, which took place nearly 2,500 years ago, does not seem all that different from one that you might read about today. What do you think?

Cast of Characters:

Milo (MEE-loh), prosecutor. He is Timotheos' son (by his first marriage), Daphne's step-son, and Leon's half-brother.

Leon (LAY-own), Daphne's defender. He is Timotheos' and Daphne's son and Milo's half brother.

Magistrate, the person who makes sure that both sides get a just trial and who keeps order in the court.

Members of the jury, the people who will decide Daphne's guilt or innocence.

Timekeeper, the person who monitors the water clock and lets the magistrate know when time is up.

Vote counters, the people who count the votes and report the results to the magistrate, who announces the verdict.

Introduction

The facts below are based on an actual murder trial that took place in Athens between 450 and 411 B.C. Just like the real trial, the outcome of this mock trial will hinge on the speeches given by the prosecutor (Milo) and the defense (Leon). Those speeches will be based on information supplied in *The Scene of the Crime* and in the Key Facts section, below.

Key Facts in the Trial of Daphne

✴ Both Timotheos and Philoneos died after their drinks were spiked with a poisonous love potion supplied by Daphne.

✴ Daphne does not deny supplying the poison that killed the two men. But she does deny knowing that it was poisonous. She says that she believed it was a true love potion.

✴ The person who sold Daphne the love potion cannot be found.

✴ Love potions are a commonly sold item in Athens, so it is not unusual that a wife would give one to her husband.

Murder in Athens! Part III (cont.)

✳ Daphne has refused to allow her slaves to be questioned by the authorities about buying the love potion. (Under Athenian law, all slaves who witnessed a crime had to be questioned under torture. Many people believed that only a slave who was tortured would tell the truth.)

✳ Milo says that his dying father claimed that he was deliberately poisoned by Daphne. However, nobody else heard Timotheos say that.

✳ Milo also says that on a previous occasion, Timotheos caught Daphne preparing a "love potion" that was actually poison. Again, no other person can confirm Milo's story.

Instructions

The following tips are designed to help both sides prepare their speeches. Remember, they are only suggestions. If other arguments are used, make sure they follow the facts of the case outlined in *The Scene of the Crime* and in the Key Facts section.

Ten Tips for Milo (Daphne's prosecutor)

✳ Point out what a good man Timotheos was, how much you loved him as a father, and how much he suffered before his death.

✳ Explain how much grief you have gone through because of losing your father.

✳ Point out how treacherous it is for a wife to kill her husband.

✳ Point out that Daphne was having marital trouble with Timotheos before she gave him the poison.

✳ Point out that the person who supplied Daphne with the love potion cannot be found now, which is suspicious.

✳ Point out that Daphne refused to let her slaves be questioned under torture (such questioning is customary in cases like this).

✳ Admit that you cannot prove conclusively that Daphne knew the love potion was poisonous. However, the fact that she poisoned him during a time of marital difficulty is extremely suspicious. It is hard to believe that his death was just a coincidence.

✳ Tell the jury that before he died, Timotheos told you that he believed that Daphne deliberately poisoned him. Also, one time before, he had caught her trying to slip him

Murder in Athens! Part III (cont.)

a poisonous drink that she called a "love potion."

✷ Undermine Leon's credibility. Point out that he is defending his mother (Daphne) and will probably say anything to save her.

✷ Point out that just because a murderer is clever and covers her trail does not mean that she should be allowed to get away with the crime.

Ten Tips for Leon (Daphne's defender)

✷ Point out that you loved and honored Timotheos because he was your father. However, unlike your half brother (Milo), you have accepted the fact that his death was accidental.

✷ Point out that Milo has no proof of his central charge—that Daphne knew she was giving the two men poison.

✷ There are many different explanations for how the men's drinks could have been poisoned. For instance, Themis could have acted on her own in slipping them poison. Or, more likely, the person who sold the love potion to Daphne gave her poison.

✷ Just because somebody is having marital problems does not mean that they will resort to murder.

✷ The fact that the person who sold the love potion to Daphne cannot be found proves nothing. In fact, it makes sense that a person who sold an unknowing person poison would try to hide.

✷ Undercut Milo's credibility. For instance, he says that Timotheos told him that Daphne deliberately poisoned him. But why didn't he share these thoughts with anyone else?

✷ Milo also says that Timotheos caught Daphne trying to poison him once before. But if that were true, why would Timotheos stay married to her and continue to trust her?

✷ Daphne did not allow her slaves to be questioned because she did not want them tortured. This shows what a caring person she is, not that she is trying to hide something.

✷ Point out that Daphne has suffered because of her husband's death and that this trial has only increased her suffering.

✷ Remind the jury that if they convict Daphne she will be executed. If they later find out that they are wrong, they will have been guilty of murder themselves.

Trial Props:
The Water Clock and the Ballot
⮱ Ancient Inventions and Innovations ⮲

Timing is Everything: The Water Clock

Since they didn't have modern timepieces, Athenians used a water clock, or *klepsydra*, to time the speeches given by prosecutors and defendants. Use the following materials to make a class klepsydra for the mock trial.

MATERIALS
◈ • • • • • • • • • • •

1-liter plastic liquid container (remove the lid or cap)
bucket (must hold more fluid than plastic container)
scissors
leather punch or another small, pointed object
   (pens and pencils usually will not work)

timepiece with a second hand
paper towels
duct tape (optional)
pen or marker

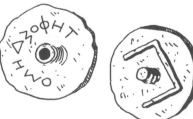

HERE'S HOW
◈ • • • • • • • • • • •

1 Punch a small hole in the base of the one-liter bottle. The opening should be small enough so that a thumb or forefinger can stop the flow of water.

2 Fill the container up, covering the opening with your finger or duct tape.

3 Set the filled bottle above an empty bucket (see illustration), open the hole, and time the water as it comes out. Be sure to put towels under the bottle and the bucket—the flow of water may be unpredictable.

4 It should take about four to six minutes for the water to drain out of the one-liter bottle. To get a precise time, mark the water level before opening the hole and write the time it took to empty by the appropriate level. Adjust the water level until you get the time you need. For this exercise, it is important only that both the prosecutor and the defense get equal time.

The Verdict Is In: The Ballot

Each Athenian juror had two ballots (see drawings). One of the wheel-like ballots had a hollow hub (a guilty vote) and the other had a solid one (a not-guilty vote). Putting one ballot in each hand, the juror covered up the two centers of each ballot with his thumb and forefinger to keep his vote secret. He would deposit one in the container used to collect votes and put the other in a discard bin. Follow this suggestion to make your own jury ballots:

Cut out two quarter-sized circles of stiff paper to make a set of one guilty and one not-guilty ballot for each student jury member. Create the guilty ballots by hole-punching the middle of the paper circles. Students can cast their votes by dropping the appropriate ballot in an assigned ballot box (or jar) and placing the other in a discard box.